Kathy Kirby
Secrets, Loves and Lip Gloss

A biography
by
James Harman

Kathy Kirby
Secrets, Loves and Lip Gloss

A biography
by
James Harman

Publisher
Mediaworld PR Ltd
Best Books Online

ISBN-10: 1-904502-90-3
ISBN-13: 978-1-904502-90-6

For my beloved mother.

Mom, you didn't live to read this,

but you witnessed every moment of it with me.

Dear Kathy,

Written with love, affection and admiration.

James

James Harman has been a professional actor for over 30 years.

With a wealth of experience, he has appeared in countless productions all around the United Kingdom, everywhere from Inverness to Southampton. He has also written three plays: the comedy thriller 'Murder Off Stage', the murder mystery 'Deadly Rivals' (a two hander concerning a fictitious meeting between Hollywood legends Joan Crawford and Bette Davis) and the highly successful 'Adults Only' comedy 'Any Extras?' which has now completed three national tours and a long summer season in Blackpool.

'Secrets, Loves and Lip Gloss' is his first book.

Contents

The star who never stopped shining-she was just hidden behind the clouds for a while. Graham Smith (Publisher)

'The sound of applause is delicious, and it's a thrill to have the world at your feet.

The praise of the crowd, well, it's exciting, but I've found it's not what makes a life complete.

There's one thing you can do for the rest of your days that's worth more than applause, the screaming crowds, the bouquets....Make someone happy...'

Kathy Kirby did just that, and continues to do so

'Fame, if you win it, well it comes and it goes in a minute. Where is the real stuff in life to cling to?'

(Make Someone Happy. Syne, Comden, Green. Publishers:-Chappell Music)

The Author and Publisher would like to thank all the artistes who have so kindly given their thoughts and memories of Kathy for the foreword of this book.
Thanks also to David Innes and Patrick Newley.

The stars turn out for a star

Paying their tributes to and sharing memories of Kathy Kirby on the following pages are:-

Vince Hill, The Bachelors, Sir Jimmy Savile OBE KCSG, Tommy Bruce, Denny Boyce, Acker Bilk, The Beverley Sisters, Jess Conrad, Anita Harris, Frank Ifield, Brenda Lee, Jeannie Mackinnon, Julie Rogers, Sandie Shaw, Stan Stennett MBE and Mark Wynter.

****

The Bachelors

The Bachelors

Why did she disappear?

Con and I, The Bachelors, seemed to be with Kathy Kirby every other week!

She seemed to always appear in summer season while we were there. She was always one week ahead or behind us on the nationwide tours. A lovely girl, I admit I fancied her like mad...but who didn't?

She wasn't the racy, over glamorous person that the lip gloss implied. She was quiet and kept herself private. I can say I never once saw her at a party, and there were many.

We played Blackpool when she played the ABC with Frank Ifield, now that was a formidable bill. Yes, our theatre was packed each night and so was theirs. But then they were the halcyon days of live showbiz, two shows a night for 16 weeks, unheard of these days.

Why did Kathy fade and almost disappear? Another mystery of the universe. Some say she quit at the top, a smart move, but hey, I was with Dame Vera Lynn the other week at Glynd Palace, she is 88 later this year.

We would love to see Kathy present herself to the public, she is missed, and I feel she would be shocked at how well the public would welcome her back.

We love you Kathy! You are a shining star in the firmament of show business. You are an icon.

'Icons are the living ones-legends are mostly dead!'
(Lauren Bacall)

Regards
Dec and Con Cluskey (The Bachelors)

The day Kathy became a Beverley Sister!

Of course we remember working with Kathy, she was a lovely lady with a great voice. One time when one of us was ill we had a live Kathy Kirby Show to film. We always sing as a threesome and Kathy offered to step in. We went on stage, the three of us, and it actually worked well. People thought it was a spoof, and to some extent it was.

Kathy was a good looking girl and a great singer, it is a very happy memory for us.

We are delighted to pay tribute to this great star.

The Beverley Sisters

Kathy as the third Beverley sister (extreme left)

My best memory of Kathy is of when we were both on the same
television show and Kathy was singing her hit 'Acapulco 22'.
Instead of singing Acapulco she sang 'Acker Bilko 22' much to
everyone's amusement.
She is a lovely lady.

Acker Bilk

Denny Boyce

From Denny Boyce

I started my big band in 1954. The combination was four trumpets, four trombones, five saxophones, piano, bass and drums. From 1955 to 1970 we were resident, and broadcasting, from London's major ballrooms such as the Orchid Ballroom, Purley; Wimbledon Palais; Streatham Locarno; Tottenham Royal; The Empire, Leicester Square and the Lyceum.

In 1955 the proprietor of the Orchid Ballroom, where we were resident at the time, released me to undertake a six-week tour of America with a small rock band. With the great saxophonist, Geoff Taylor, as co-leader, we went on an exchange deal with Freddy and the Bell Boys coming to England.

One afternoon in 1957 a lady knocked on my door in Ilford, Essex. She had a very pretty, young girl with her. She told me it was her daughter and that she was a very good singer, and would I listen to her?

I did, and she was, and she joined us at the Wimbledon Palais immediately, and later moved on with us to the Lyceum. She always knocked everybody out with her appearance, power and personality.

Kathy Kirby was a true professional. Always on time for rehearsals and word perfect, she was a joy to work with. I was not at all surprised that she became the most popular and highest paid singer of her time.

Denny Boyce

Tommy Bruce, another Stars and Garters star

My memories of Kathy are of a lovely young girl with a wonderful voice, who matured into a beautiful woman.If you met Kathy you couldn't help but fall under her spell, it was always a pleasure to be in her company.

Being on Stars and Garters was a lot of fun and working with Kathy made it even more of a fun place to be. She had a warm and welcoming personality, add to that her stunning good looks and powerful singing voice, and you had the perfect recipe for success. I took as much pleasure as any of the fans in listening to her and watching her perform.

I am sorry that circumstances in her private life have deprived us all of seeing and hearing her for some time now. Her absence from the scene is a great loss to those of us who loved working with her, as well as to her fans.

I miss her very much, and wish her pleasure and happiness in all aspects of her life in the future. This book is long overdue and I look forward to reading it.

Tommy Bruce

From Jess Conrad

Then...and now!

In 1966 I toured South Africa with Kathy Kirby and we did many UK engagements afterwards.

I know it has been said before, but Kathy was truly the most glamorous of our female singing stars. Our tour of South Africa was a tremendous success, we looked sensational together, and it wasn't long before we were completely besotted with each other. The only thing standing in her way was her manager and guru/boyfriend at the time, Ambrose.

One night I slipped a triple sleeping pill into his brandy, and, while he slept for 12 hours, Kathy and I partied.

It was probably an unforgiveable thing to do, but we were young and foolish. Looking back at those days it was a bit like a holiday romance, but a very special one.

Soon afterwards I went into West End musicals, Jesus in Godspell and Joseph in Joseph and His Technicolour Dreamcoat, and lost touch with Kathy.

I am delighted that this book has finally been written about her, somebody who was so close to so many people's hearts, especially mine.

Jess Conrad

Anita Harris

Kathy had an endearing quality and, at times, resembled Monroe in looks and body language. You see that in the cover of this book. We met many times on "the rounds" and I admired her greatly. She expressed lyrics wonderfully, particularly songs of emotion. Singing a new song on its first performance is about presenting the composer's combination of notes and words and how to best express their meaning and musical intention. Sometimes, it is also about putting a new twist on the delivery of a familiar song. Kathy will be remembered as much for her artistry in those areas as for her beauty, her emotion and her generous heart.

Anita Harris

Vince Hill

'I first met Kathy Kirby when I was doing a TV series in the mid-sixties, called Stars and Garters.

From the moment she walked through the door there was no doubting that she was destined to be a star. The blonde hair, the boobs, the lip gloss- the whole image was of a British Marilyn Monroe. She was every man's fantasy woman.

The show was live and required one's full concentration to get through what we had to get through each week, so, although we all got to know each other, we didn't have too much time to get 'up close and personal' as they say!

Apart from that we were all doing other things- and as far as I was concerned, I was doing a radio series called Parade of the Pops, as well as various one nighters and TV commercials and guesting on other radio shows.

However, you didn't need to spend much time with Kathy to see that she simply radiated stardom. She always knew she would be a star and she was. But that kind of talent needs strong handling and the two people in her life who took care of that were her agent, Evie Taylor, and her manager, who I think really discovered her, Ambrose, the bandleader with whom she sang in her early days. He was her guide and mentor I feel. Evie Taylor, her agent, was also a force to be reckoned with!

And so she was propelled to stardom, to her own TV series- hit records (the biggest being 'Secret Love'of course). She was the girl of the moment, the 'IT' girl of her time.

This is just my personal 'gut feeling', but I think that when Ambrose died, something in Kathy died too. A spark went out, and sadly for all of us it was never to be rekindled. Perhaps, perhaps this book may re-light the fire.

Vince Hill

Frank Ifield

My first meeting with Kathy Kirby was not exactly under the most favourable of conditions. The year was 1960 and we were booked along with singer Jimmy Lloyd and Alan Randal, the George Formby impressionist and vibraphone player, as support acts on the 'Emile Ford Show' in a series of one nighters. The tour was to open with an afternoon matinee. We all arrived in good time, but by the start of the first show, Emile and his band, the Checkmates, had not turned up. We believed the Checkmates would be providing the musical backing for the show – but unfortunately it seems someone forgot to mention this fact to them! Nevertheless, the show had to go on. The curtain went up with Alan Randal on the piano and me on guitar providing a hurriedly improvised backing.

Kathy was very shy offstage, and the last minute panic was all very upsetting for her. But the minute she stepped foot on stage, she shone like a beacon and her melodic voice had the power to stop you in your tracks.

We were both just young aspiring artists in those days who were beginning to get a few breaks, yet working alongside Kathy, I felt confident that even the toughest audiences would come away entertained despite neither of us having the benefit of hit records. The next time I recall us being together was supporting American star guitarist, Duane Eddy. Like myself, Kathy was beginning to forge ahead, gaining a following in her own right with lots of TV appearances.

After that, although I was aware of what she was doing, we were not booked to work together until the summer of 1964 at the ABC Theatre in Blackpool, this time as stars of the show. By then, I'd had my big number one hit 'I Remember You' followed by more chart toppers and Kathy was herself a recording star, having earned herself a chart position in August of 1963 with her brilliant vocal version of the Shadows composition "Dance On", followed up in November with the even more successful "Secret Love" and, in February of 64, her top ten hit 'Let Me Go Lover'. Yet, although she was now a well established artiste, she was still the same unassuming and rather shy person I had first met three years earlier. It was a pleasure to work again with her and it was hardly surprising, given the fact that we were both highly successful recording stars, that we broke the box office record for that year.

I have written much more about Kathy and the shows we did together in my newly published autobiography 'I Remember Me' – and there's a great photo of Kathy in there, too."

Frank Ifield

Brenda Lee

I had the great pleasure of working with Kathy on the Royal Variety Show for the Queen. I believe the year was 1964.

She was such a star, but more than that, she was so sweet and down to earth, which was unusual for someone of her stature.

She made me feel so welcome and I appreciated that quality in her. She made such wonderful contributions to our world of music, and left all of us, her fans, some precious memories.

Brenda Lee

The legendary Wilson, Kepple and Betty with Jeannie
Mackinnon, the last 'Betty' of the act

Ah, Kathy Kirby - what memories! I only had the opportunity to work with Kathy on one occasion in the late fifties, before she became a big star, but what a happy and enjoyable time it was.

I was in Manchester for a week of variety. The boys and I were closing the first half with an American recording star topping the bill. Sorry, but I can't remember who it was that particular week, we worked with so many. I do remember though that Bruce Forsyth was our main opposition that week at another theatre.

Kathy and I were the only girls on our bill and hit it off immediately. We even decided to share digs together. My memories are of a strawberry blonde who worked really hard at her profession, and obviously had the talent to be a star-something that she really longed for.

A perfectionist, she noticed that I toured my Grundy reel-to-reel tape recorder with me. Kathy got me to record her act on several occasions from the dressing room show relay. There was no ego or vanity in this, she simply wanted to listen to herself working.

Very self critical she was, always seeking to improve her work. Ambitious? Yes. I remember her act in those days included the Peggy Lee classic 'Mr Wonderful' and 'Come Rain, Come Shine', which brought the house down every night.

She was also a shopaholic! We went shopping in Manchester on several occasions and she was always keen to browse the make up counter. I have never seen anyone buy so many lipsticks in one shopping spree!

A lovely young girl with no pretensions, she simply knew what her dream was and went for it.

My most vivid memory is of Bruce Forsyth inviting Joe, Jack, me and Kathy over to his hotel for an after show meal one night. I remember Bruce spent most of the evening playing piano for us, with Kathy occassionally joining him with a song. It was obvious even in those days that she had undefinable 'star quality'. I guess she probably still has it all these years later. When you are touched by angels with that kind of talent it is unlikely you ever loose it.

Jeannie Mackinnon

Julie Rogers

Kathy and I never met, as you will understand that we were never booked on the same shows for obvious reasons, but it is strange that our backgrounds were very similar, having both come via the 'big bands, and having band leaders as our managers.

In Kathy's case it was Ambrose and in mine Teddy Foster, who at one time had worked for Ambrose.

Kathy, I believe, had her first hit a little before me-I think in about 1963, but it brought in the "big ballads" for girls. She brought great glamour to the scene, which personally I loved, rather than the 'girl next door' look.

I've continued to work and tour up to the present time and I think that it's a great shame we haven't seen more of Kathy. She always appeared to me to be a very nice person.

Julie Rogers

Sir Jimmy Savile

Kathy Kirby was always, to me, a special person. Meeting her as a teenage patron of my dance hall in London, I was immediately struck by her vital looks and personality.

She told me she wanted to be a singer and I explained to her that it was a hard life, not an easy one. This mattered to Kathy not at all, and over the months of her coming into my dance hall she would ply me with questions and I would try to give her the answers. The rest is history because she met up with, I think, Bert Ambrose, and I understand he suggested singing lessons and she eventually came to be the superstar that we all know.

I was always very happy to have known her as a teenage patron with ambition and very happy that she achieved what she wanted so much.

Sir Jimmy Savile OBE KCSG

One of the highlights of my life was visiting Kathy while she was hospitalised after her breakdown.

Being a star does not make you immune from problems. She couldn't wait to get out of what she called "the bin", and put her mink coats and lip gloss on again.

I must say I got to know her much better when she was not well, and no longer performing for everyone else's benefit.

We all knew that Kathy had a very unhappy start to her professional life, but she was protected from meeting anyone who might sympathise or offer an alternative to her sad, lonely lifestyle.

Sandie Shaw

Stan Stennett

There can be no higher compliment from one professional to another than to say 'What A Performer!' That is something I can truly say about Kathy Kirby.

Our paths in showbusiness did not cross too often, indeed, I think we probably only did one Sunday concert together, but that did not stop me from being a very big fan – then and now.

When I was working in panto with Eric Morecambe and Ernie Wise we often spoke of her work. She was Britain's answer to the great Miss Peggy Lee. She had a voice that was quite unlike any other at the time, full of emotion and power. It was a great shame that she did not continue to perform longer than she did.

Her time with Bert Ambrose and his orchestra – one of the great band leaders of our time – will long be remembered.

Fortunately the great British public still has her recordings available to enjoy. During my time when presenting radio shows, I often included examples of her work, and she was amongst a group of favourites of mine that included Ruby Murray, Dusty Springfield, Lita Roza, Anne Shelton and Joan Regan etc.

She looked and sounded like an angel and I hope she will take great pleasure from knowing that she still has so many devoted fans.

Stan Stennett MBE.

Mark Wynter

In my mid-teens the image of Kathy Kirby suggested beauty and glamorous sex appeal. A few years down the line when we worked together in various television shows, I realised Kathy was much more than that. A woman of warmth and quality with a dramatic and powerful edge to her voice.

Conversely I sensed a frailty and vulnerability in her persona that was almost childlike.

As an outstanding vocalist of the British Big Band era, who achieved successful pop singer status, her bright light was dimmed all too soon. However, a little of something special gives more lasting pleasure than many of today's transient, pyrotechnic song thrushes.

Kathy's talent and presence represented intangible star quality.

Mark Wynter

Introduction

"Over the past years I have had many great singers in my band, including Hildegarde, Vera Lynn and Anne Shelton, but I have never known anyone with everything that Kathy has to offer- voice, tone, range feeling, personality and looks. In fact this girl has it all, and nothing can stop her becoming one of the greatest stars of our time."

Bert Ambrose

****

Kathy Kirby…blonde and blue-eyed, the busty glamour girl of song, possessed one of the finest female singing voices the United Kingdom has ever produced.

With lips moistly parted, she sang rather old-fashioned songs in cleavage revealing beaded dresses.

She was called Britain's answer to Marilyn Monroe. She certainly wasn't typical of the "Swinging 60s" in fashion or song, yet she rapidly became one of the decade's biggest stars, and was indeed the highest paid girl singer of the 1960s.

For a few years it was impossible to turn on the radio without a disc jockey playing one of her records, or to switch on the television without seeing her belting out one of her hit numbers.

Nicknamed both "The Golden Girl of Pop" and "Queen of British Television", at the pinnacle of her success she could do no wrong.

Top Ten hit records, major TV series which attracted vast viewing figures, a Royal Variety appearance, top flight summer seasons, and sell out concert and cabaret tours, in this country and abroad. Yet by the time the 1980s arrived she was attempting one comeback after another at smaller and smaller venues, at one point appearing at a Kent bingo hall, singing between each game.

What went so horribly wrong for her? How could such a remarkable talent go to waste? Was she the victim of circumstance and corruption, or did she self-destruct, unable to cope with her vast fame?

After years of much personal heartache in the 70s, she decided to tell her story to a leading newspaper at the beginning of 1980. It ended with her words: *"If I am no longer the glossy lipped, golden girl of pop, I still have one asset left-that is my voice. I am not going to write my career off. Someone, somewhere will surely give me that one chance I need."*

Many people in many places did just that, including myself. In the end, I, like everyone else, walked away. I didn't return for some years. Perhaps the reasons for that will become clear during the course of this book. A book that tells a story which you quite simply could not make up.

James Harman 2005

Chapter One

Singer With The Band

"Mr Ambrose, can I sing with your band please?"

Kathy Kirby

I

Kathy Kirby was born Kathleen O'Rourke on October 20th 1938 in Ilford, Essex, not 1940 as is widely thought. She was the eldest of three children, and her mother Eileen struggled to give Kathy, her sister Pat, and brother Douglas, a good upbringing after their father left home when they were very young. Eileen O'Rourke was a strong, dominating Irish woman with a quick temper, who readily assumed charge of the house and made sure her children did not go without.

Eileen first spotted that Kathy had talent when she entered, and won, her first talent contest, at the tender age of three. The youngster belted out "Oh Johnny" and was rewarded with a box of colouring crayons.

Educated at the Ursaline Convent School, where she naturally became a member of the choir, Kathy's talent was nurtured by Eileen. From the age of nine she paid for her eldest daughter to have private singing lessons. Kathy's main ambition at that age was to pursue a career in opera. However, when she was twelve, she discovered pop music and set her sights on becoming a singer of more modern music. A pop singer, but with one small provision; the young girl had decided she was going to be a star with all the trappings that it entailed.

Throughout those early days Kathy and her sister entered many local talent competitions, occasionally singing duets. During this period Kathy won many certificates at music festivals, and soon realised that she preferred singing alone rather than sharing centre stage. Knowing she was good and that audiences seemed to like her voice, she bided her time until an opportunity presented itself.

At 16, with her natural red hair dyed blonde and school behind her, Kathy and Pat spent their free evenings at Ilford's Palais de Danse. One night the two of them walked into the dance hall to discover the legendary bandleader Bert Ambrose was appearing with his band.

II

Bert Ambrose was Britain's top dance bandleader of the 30s and 40s. However, the rapidly changing face of popular music in the late 1950s mirrored Ambrose's decline.

He realised that his style of music was becoming dated and that his touring days would soon be at and end. Looking around the Palais that night he could see all the youngsters who had discovered the attraction of rock'n'roll.

Kathy, however, knew the band was good, and was determined to ask Ambrose for an audition. Wearing a tight, black, shiny dress, black evening gloves, and carrying a nine-inch long cigarette holder (she didn't smoke), she asked him if she could sing with his band.

Amused at the sight of this over-made up kid, Ambrose bent down to talk to her. With a faint smile he asked her which song she wanted to sing.

"Love Me or Leave Me," said Kathy.

"What key?" asked Ambrose.

"Any key," came the reply, "I've been singing a long time," said an indignant Kathy.

Well, for whatever reason, Ambrose gave her the chance she wanted.

Minutes later she was on stage belting out the old torch number. Although she finished ahead of the band she received a tremendous ovation from the crowd, so much so that she followed it with another song, a powerful rendition of the old standard 'All Of Me'.

Ambrose could see all too clearly how the young audience responded to Kathy's numbers. Maybe it might not be such a bad idea to have a vocalist with his band who was much nearer to the age group they were playing to. Besides, he recognised that this very pretty girl had real talent, no matter how raw.

Speaking to Ambrose after her brief moment of glory, Kathy, after adding two years to her age, was told to come back the following night with her mother. Kathy duly did this with mother, Eileen, in tow. Kathy's mother, of course, knew of the legendary bandleader's reputation and, after giving his personal assurance that he would look after the aspiring singer, a contract was signed at a rate of £10 a week and Kathy was set to tour with the band for the rest of the 13-week run. It would prove to be 13 weeks of invaluable experience.

III

On the road Kathy soon learned that winning local competitions was totally different to being a professional band singer. Ambrose coached her how to stand in front of a microphone and look relaxed, how to use her hands and arms to create the best effect, how to stand and place her feet, how to dress, how to make up and how to get the best out of her voice. She learned the all important breath control so that she could hold a top C sharp for eight seconds.

Kathy's working relationship stretched far beyond the 13 weeks, which she had initially signed for. She toured the country with Ambrose, until he eventually dismantled the band. Soon afterwards she got a job singing at a restaurant in Madrid. Engaged to appear for a month, her contract was extended, and she stayed for almost five months.

Back home she then toured with Nat Allen and Denny Boyce's bands before stepping out in 1960 as an artiste in her own right. She supported Cliff Richard on tour, sang at The Astor, and all the other top London nightclubs. It was a long, exhausting apprenticeship, but, as she said, she could not have learned the ropes any other way.

However, with the months turning into years, there was still no sign of her breaking through into the big time, to find the fame she longed for so desperately.

IV

Becoming more and more restless, she telephoned Ambrose. Depressed, Kathy told him that she was still scratching around for a living and was thinking of giving up on her career. During the conversation she told him about a forthcoming date at Wimbledon Palais. Ambrose, out of curiosity, made a note of the date and went along to hear her sing once more. He was stunned by the progress she had made since he had last seen her. No longer a raw beginner – in fact much more than a competent band singer – he saw that besides the thrilling voice and stunning looks, she had created a quite unique presence under the spotlight.

Very soon after the engagement Kathy and Ambrose signed a contract for him to become her manager, starting at £25 a week, with Ambrose taking 15% of all outside fees. It was the beginning of a relationship that would bring Kathy international fame, wealth, adulation – and ultimately heartache, disaster and immense personal pain.

Chapter Two

'Stars And Garters' And Fame

"I was brought up in a comfortable, average, middle class home, but I knew when I was quite young that I wanted to rise above the average. As I found, more and more, that people liked my singing, I realised my voice was my most likely passport to fame,"

Kathy Kirby

I

Singing with Ambrose was a big step forward for Kathy, but it did not mean that instant success was around the corner. Certainly Ambrose was a celebrated figure in London's West End, but his contacts were not what they once were, and a new breed of agents, musicians and impresarios were sweeping into the capital's nightlife.

So had he a good girl singer? There were plenty of good girl singers around.

Ambrose booked Kathy into various small London clubs, of which there were plenty, and continued to groom and train her. She also had to learn to deal with the late night audiences, many times the worse for drink. Then…a lucky break.

One of the larger, upmarket nightclubs had booked a female singer from America. Opening the season with a good deal of pre-show publicity, the management soon discovered that she was not worth her fee. Soon after the opening, the club asked Kathy to take her place.

Ambrose hesitated, however, not sure it would be such a good move. Although Kathy was an experienced band singer, could she win over a sophisticated "seen it all" supper club audience so early in her career?

Reluctantly, he finally agreed to Kathy appearing, but, not able to stand the tension, when she walked on stage, he took refuge in the manager's office! After a while curiosity got the better of him and, taking a peep through the crack in the door, saw that Kathy was indeed slaying them.

II

Now 21, Kathy had built up a good reputation as a cabaret singer, not only in Britain but also in Spain and Portugal. She had signed a recording contract with Pye International, and, although the two records she had released on that label, "Love Can Be" and "Danny", achieved some airplay on the radio they failed to make any impression on the charts.

She finally got her television break with a spot on "The Arthur Haynes Show" for the commercial network, and soon after had other guest appearances including "Cool for Cats".

It was all starting to fall into place.

The co-producers of a new variety series, John Hamilton and

Daphne Shadwell, spotted Kathy's TV appearances and were more than impressed. The series they were planning for Associated Rediffusion was to be called 'Stars and Garters', which they hoped would capture the happy atmosphere of a night out at a local pub.

Kathy was immediately offered one of the resident singing spots on the show. 'Stars and Garters' made its television debut on Friday May 31st 1963. Although it started with the minimum of publicity, within weeks the programme became a firm favourite with millions of viewers throughout the UK. The show was hosted by camp comedian, Ray Martine, and Kathy shared the numbers with Vince Hill, Tommy Bruce and Clinton Ford.

From the first programme the fan mail began to filter in for Kathy, and by the end of the first series it was obvious from the volume of mail who had become the main attraction of the show. As John Hamilton and Daphne Shadwell have since said: "Stars and Garters will always be memorable because of Kathy Kirby."

III

During the previous year, Ambrose, unhappy with Kathy's recording contract with Pye, arranged for her to sign with the company that had been the outlet for his own discs over the decades, Decca. Her first record for the company was 'Bigman', released on October 26th 1962. Although it received healthy reviews, and a good amount of airtime, selling in the end around 50,000 copies, it failed to make an entry into the charts. However, the follow up recording finally enabled Kathy to achieve one of her ambitions, to record a hit song. Her vocal version of the Shadows' previous Christmas instrumental hit 'Dance On' entered the charts on August 15th, where it remained for the next 11 weeks, climbing eventually to number 11 in the Top 20.

Kath also had the good news that 'Dance On' charted in Australia; somewhere she was to have considerable success in cabaret later in the decade. In the end it sold around a quarter of a million copies in this country alone, and her next release was about to double that figure and give her the song that she has become most associated with. Indeed it became her theme music. 'Secret Love'.

Meanwhile, besides her regular appearances on 'Stars and Garters', she was guesting on all the top pop shows of the day. Programmes like 'Ready, Steady, Go' and the Birmingham made 'Thank Your Lucky Stars'. Headline appearances at cabaret venues across the country filled her diary, her name was now on people's lips and she was almost there.

IV

"I have never met anyone with such tremendous versatility and capabilities. Perhaps it is her ability to switch styles with such ease that impressed me most. First she would evoke the Music Hall atmosphere of Vesta Tilley's era, and immediately switch into her captivating teen-appeal style for her next

number, all without any apparent effort."

Peter Sullivan (Record Producer)

Kathy's recording manager, Peter Sullivan, suggested the song that would be her biggest success. A long time Doris Day fan, Kathy was asked about recording Day's 'Secret Love' with an up-tempo beat. Kathy always loved the number and she jumped at the chance. It proved to be a wise suggestion; crashing into the charts on the 7th November 1963. During an 18-week stay it eventually reached number 4, only being denied top spot by two recordings by the Beatles and one from Cliff Richard. Consolation was that the song earned her a Silver Disc for its sales and £30,000 in royalties for this record alone.

It seemed to the viewing public that rarely a week went by without her being featured on some television show or other. During the week 'Secret Love' stood at number 5, Kathy appeared on 'Thank Your Lucky Stars' on the Saturday evening, to be followed on the Sunday with her debut appearance on 'Sunday Night At The London Palladium'. The following Wednesday she would be returning to the small screen for a new series of 'Stars and Garters', and now there would be no doubt who was the main star. Just weeks before she had been the subject of Alan Freeman's series, 'Here Come The Girls'. The programme highlighted a different girl singer each week, and it must have been of great satisfaction to both Kathy and Ambrose that her particular show achieved the highest figures for the whole series.

It was during the run of the first series of 'Stars and Garters' that I became a fan. As an eleven year old I fell totally in love with her. A throw back to the glamour girls of Hollywood and she also had this wonderful voice. I decorated my bedroom with her photographs, bought her records and became a member of her fan club in May 1964. (then run by Valerie Hopkins). I just couldn't get enough of her.

James Harman.

Naturally with Kathy's star growing daily, plans were made for her to record a long-playing record. The aim was to have it rush-released in time for the Christmas market. 'Kathy Kirby Sings Hits From Stars and Garters' entered the charts in the first week of the New Year and stayed for the next eight weeks, reaching number 11.

In many ways 1964 was to be Kathy's most successful year. Following the success of 'Secret Love', the New Year began with the release of the follow-up single. 'Let Me Go Lover' had previously been a hit in the USA for both Joan Weber and Teresa Brewer, and over in this country with Ruby Murray. Recorded in January and released on the 14th February into 10th position it stayed for 11 weeks. Kathy was to state that she was surprised that 'Lover' had done so well. *"I don't like it as much as Secret Love and when I made it I thought it might never get anywhere at all."*

V

It was in January of 1964 that I had my first opportunity of seeing Kathy 'live'. She was engaged as one of the guests at the Birmingham Rotary Club's annual celebrity concert, at the Alexandra Theatre. It was to be held on the last Sunday in the month, and other artists on the bill would include Ronnie Carroll, The Three Monarchs and Nicholas Parsons. I can remember that night as if it were yesterday. Kathy closed the first half and I, not being able to settle during the interval, was taken home by my mother. We missed the entire second half, not that I could have cared. J.H.

Following her appearance at the Alexandra Theatre further spots on just about all the major television variety shows followed. Programmes such as the BBC's 'Billy Cotton Show' and ITV 'A Touch Of The Norman Vaughans'. Stage shows included an appearance at the Royal Albert Hall for the Baird Festival and 'The Ready, Steady, Go Mod Ball' at the Empire Pool, at which around 8,000 teenagers were admitted. Also on the bill were The Rolling Stones, Cilla Black and The Searchers. One further highlight was an appearance on the New Musical Express Poll Winners Concert staged at the Empire Pool, Wembley. It was here that Kathy was awarded her trophy for Best British Female Singer of 1963. Second billed only to Cliff Richard and The Shadows, as the New Musical Express reported at the time; "If Kathy Kirby had just stood on stage in her black two-piece suit without singing a note, that would have been quite enough for myself and the rest of the boys. But she pleased everyone with a dynamic performance of 'You're The One' backed by Joe Loss. She followed with the jaunty 'Acapulco 22' and had the thousands of teenagers hand clapping to the rhythm.'

'You're the One' incidentally would become her new record. Recorded in May 1964, it entered the charts in July of that year and reached number 17 during a stay of nine weeks.

Through this time Ambrose was having secret negotiations with the BBC with the view to Kathy recording a one-off special. Having decided not to sign with Rediffusion for another series, Kathy didn't want to become simply the 'blonde with the shiny lips from that pub programme'. The star and her manager felt the show had served its purpose in getting Kathy into the public eye. Ambrose's talks led to an agreement with the BBC, as a result Kathy recorded her first 'Kathy Kirby Show' in April, to be broadcast the following month.

Sunday May 3rd was the day in question. Guest artistes included the actor Stratford Johns (then riding high from Z Cars), the Italian tenor, Carlo Dini, and Peter Gordeno and his Dancers. Days before, however, Kathy had opened her first major summer season, co-starring with Frank Ifield in 'Holiday Startime' at the luxurious ABC Theatre in Blackpool, and she found herself on the front pages of all the national newspapers. The BBC chiefs had seen a preview of the forthcoming TV Special and immediately offered Ambrose a contract for eighteen further shows at £1,000 per show. At this time it was the biggest deal of its kind. Kathy at once became television's highest paid female star. Strangely enough though, she almost missed it. Ambrose was also having talks again with Rediffusion for her to star in their own thirteen-week series, to begin filming once the Blackpool season had finished. He was about to sign with the ITV company when the BBC offer was made.

The BBC special, in which she was off screen for only two minutes, was a tremendous success, both with the critics and in the ratings. She sang, danced, acted as compere and then appeared in the comedy sketches. The show was compared, by more than one reviewer, as reminiscent of one of the old Hollywood MGM musicals. All agreed though, the chief asset for the show's success was the star herself.

She had arrived. No longer just another pop artiste, but the genuine article. A star.

Chapter Three

The Golden Girl Of British Television

"For as long as I can remember I dreamed of being a famous, glamorous star."

Kathy Kirby

I

The season at Blackpool was a huge success. Kathy closed the first half of the show, happily looking forward to beginning her series with the BBC in the October. The New Musical Express takes up the story. "She opened with a fast number, 'Let Me Sing and I'm Happy' followed by a belting version of 'No Regrets', then a hand clapping 'Acapulco 22'. She continued with 'I Wish You Love', before a medley of her hits. She put her all into 'Can't Help Lovin' Dat Man of Mine' and earned terrific applause for this. One of those affording her warm acclaim was Gracie Fields, who enjoyed the show from the front of the circle. Kathy's final number brought on the entire company as she belted out in great style the Lennon and McCartney favourite 'Can't Buy Me Love'. Finishing the run in Blackpool, Kathy went directly into rehearsals for her BBC series.

The first show aired in October with the experienced television producer Ernest Maxim at the helm.

Guests on the first show included the comedy actor Bernard Bresslaw and the legendary musical comedy star Jessie Matthews. Miss Matthews was finding fame a second time around as radio's 'Mrs Dale' in 'Mrs Dale's Diary'.

I remember this particular show vividly. Kathy was on camera singing with Miss Matthews, a medley of the star's hits from her film and stage career. As the orchestra began to play the number most associated with Jessie, 'My Heart Stood Still', Kathy, putting a finger to her mouth and quietly saying 'hush' backed off screen to let the older star – who many consider to be the finest musical comedy star we have ever produced – to take centre stage alone. It was a magical moment. Kathy recorded six shows for the BBC that autumn, with a further twelve planned for the following year. Future guests would include Lonnie Donnegan, Tom Jones, The Beverley Sisters, Buddy Greco, Billy Fury, Val Doonican, and the American pianist, Peter Nero. I saved my pocket money and travelled down to London on one occasion to see the show at the Television Centre, Shepherds Bush, where that week the guest star was the international opera singer Adele Leigh.

JH

II

Before 1964 closed Kathy made two television appearances, which really consolidated her success. On the 2nd November she appeared on the stage of the London Palladium for the Royal Variety Performance. The bill topper for that year was the American singing star Lena Horne. During rehearsals Mis Horne took Kathy on one side and told her that she had caught Kathy's latest BBC show on television in her hotel room the previous Saturday evening. Kathy was thrilled when the American legend told her how wonderful she thought her singing and artistry.

Kathy also took part in a section introduced by the veteran broadcaster David Jacobs. Four girl singers sang back to back, first making their respective entrances on the Palladium's famous revolving stage in glamorous sports cars. Opening the proceedings was Cilla Black, to be followed by Millicent Martin. Kathy appeared next, in a dark green Triumph Vitesse convertible, before walking to the front of the stage in a sparkling white lurex dress, to sing 'Secret Love', Brenda Lee, the American singer known as 'Little Miss Dynamite', closed the section with a superb rendition of 'All The Way'.

The following day however, the front pages of the nationals didn't carry Miss Lee or the show's official star Lena Horne, but splashed across the covers was Kathy herself, dropping a curtsey to the Royal box.

The second major television appearance was an invitation to a ninety-minute cavalcade of entertainment on the BBC to celebrate the 90th birthday of Sir Winston Churchill. The show was broadcast on the 29th November, the eve of Sir Winston's birthday, and featured a galaxy of stars, including a rare appearance by Noel Coward. Kathy was asked to sing Marie Lloyd's music hall number 'My Old Man Said Follow The Van'. Dressed for the part, complete with birdcage, Kathy would include the routine in her stage act until the mid-seventies. Again all the national papers carried photographs of Kathy in the part over the weekend the show was broadcast.

III

Her next Decca single was released in the October. It would prove to be the first record of hers not to make the charts. The tale behind the recording of it has an interesting story of its own. During the Blackpool season, she was obviously thinking of her follow-up record to 'You're The One', besides the imminent BBC series. The track she had made was of a French melody with English lyrics; Kathy liked it very much. However, just before the release date, up to Blackpool raced Kathy's recording manager Peter Sullivan. Because of copyright problems the Kirby single had to be withdrawn before any copies could be sold. Sullivan had to find a new number for Kathy in a hurry. The two of them poured over dozens of possible songs before they came across an American number called 'Walk Away'. Kathy liked the number, but the title was changed to 'Don't Walk Away', due to the recent Matt Monro hit record of the same name.

Kathy flew down from Blackpool to London one free Sunday to record it. Reviews were mixed, all generally agreeing that perhaps the 'A' side should have been her sensational rendition of Piaf's 'No Regrets', which appeared on the flip side.

The singer rounded off what had been a wonderful year by appearing for the first time on the recently opened BBC2. In the Christmas edition of 'Open House' she topped the bill with Joe Brown.

IV

At the beginning of 1965 there could be very few residents of the UK between the ages of eight and eighty who had not heard of Kathy Kirby. This New Year would see her rise to even greater heights and to the very top of the show business ladder. The year started with the announcement that the singer had been selected to represent this country in the Eurovision Song Contest. In those days the contest was still a major television event, which attracted huge audiences.

A major change took place in selecting the United Kingdom entry this particular year. Six specially commissioned songs were written with Kathy in mind and for the first year the voting had been thrown wide open. Viewers of The Kathy Kirby Show being asked to judge themselves which should be the winning number. Formerly the decision had been made by selected regional panels from around the country. So, at the end of January, introduced by David

Jacobs, Kathy sang the six possibilities during the course of her show. Kathy, the first girl singer to represent the UK since Patricia Bredin in 1957, drew the song titles from a hat before the show began to decide the running order of the entries. At the end of the programme Kathy and David Jacobs viewed a monitor and saw the entire six numbers performed again so that the viewers could finally decide.

A number of newspapers carried the story the following day, of the contest and that the BBC chiefs had vetoed the choice of dress Kathy had originally chosen. Too low cut and tight was the decision, and eventually Kathy elected a simple black classic look. The postal votes had to be cast in time for the next 'Kathy Kirby Show', to be broadcast on February 12th, when the winning songs were to be announced. An extended player of all the songs was rush-released and obviously the winning entry would be Kathy's new single. Out of half a million postal votes the winning song proved to be 'I Belong', written by Peter Lee Stirling and Phil Peters. It received support from 110,945 viewers. Runner-up was 'I'll Try Not To Cry' by Les Reed and Barry Mason, and third was 'My Only Love' by Tom Springfield, brother of Dusty.

A few weeks later, in the edition of her show which was to be screened immediately prior to Kathy flying to Naples for the contest, the guest was the American, Stubby Kaye, who departed from the script to present Kathy with a good luck present from all involved in the series. The usual finale had taken place with everyone on stage, and as usual Kathy stepped forward into the spotlight to sing her last big number of the evening. Stubby stepped forward too and told the audience that the gift, besides being for good luck, was in appreciation from all her co-workers for her professionalism, and for being so nice to work with. It was apparent that the singer was genuinely moved.

V

Naples was a spectacular setting for the tenth Eurovision Song Contest. Up until that point in its history the British had come second no less than five times, represented by such established artists as Pearl Carr and Teddy Johnson, singing 'Little Birdie', and Bryan Johnson, 'High, High, High'. In 1965 it was generally felt that with a song that was as good as any around, sung by a fabulously glamorous vocalist, the UK was in with more than a fair chance of taking the prize.

The day before the contest Kathy spoke to the English Press about her fears for the evening to come.

"I have drawn second place in the singing order. I hope the judges will not have forgotten my three minutes by the time every song has been sung," she said.

With eighteen entries, the most countries ever to have taken part up until then, certainly a better position than second would have been wished for. However, on the night, in front of an audience of over one hundred million viewers, Kathy, looking sensational, gave the number all she had. The opening of the song had been slightly changed giving it a tremendously strong start with the Kirby voice belting out 'I Belong' three times before going into the actual number. A fabulous ovation greeted her performance, and both she, Ambrose, and the BBC had high hopes that maybe this year we would do it.

The following day all the newspapers carried banner headlines telling the complete story 'Kathy Kirby the blonde, 24-year-old star was weeping as though her heart would break', said one. 'I should have won, I should have walked it' she said in between sobs, 'I know I should have been first.' She came second.

The contest was won by a petite blonde of 17, Frances Gall. Entered in fifteenth position, she walked off with the prize for Luxembourg. Backstage, after the results became known, Miss Gall was immediately at the centre of a huge row. Although she was representing Luxembourg, it was announced that she was, in fact French, and there was at that time a growing resentment of the practice of smaller countries using foreign singers. Miss Gall, in tears as she made her way to Kathy's dressing room, agreed that Kathy should have won and not been pushed into second slot. In the end it was Kathy who was comforting Miss Gall. There were those around that night who felt it should have been very much the other way round.

Speaking of her fears, which she had mentioned to reporters the night before, of being drawn so early in the contest, she went on, "I came second and I felt great. I felt the whole of the audience were with me. Frances came on much later, late enough to be remembered I suppose. After all, by the time the concert is ending, the judges and the audience, hard as they try, must obviously lose the flavour of the earlier numbers. They are warmed up. They forget. The songs begin to draw out and the crisp early ones fade from their memory. Goodness knows this is not sour grapes, but I do feel terribly dejected now." Certainly Kathy received the biggest ovation in Naples that night, and a curious incident occurred just a few months later which illustrated the impact the singer had made.

At a European television conference, and shop window, various countries, including the BBC were looking for overseas sales. One of the smaller countries had a film of a blonde, made up like Kathy, singing 'I Belong'. The European television staff who had seen the original rocked with laughter. However, the BBC delegation took a poor view of the joke until it was pointed out to them. "But this is your own TW3 satire is it not? And satire is supposed to be cruel isn't it?" The BBC did not buy that particular programme.

During Kathy's stay in Naples she received and accepted a kind invitation from Gracie Fields and her husband to have dinner with them one evening at their home in Capri, where they had long since settled. Following the contest Kathy and Ambrose flew to Israel for a very welcome three-week holiday.

'I Belong' would prove to be Kathy's last chart hit to date (although she would continue to sell well enough on Decca and later EMI for many years to come); it came into the charts on March 4[th,] reaching number 36 during a three week stay. The number also provided her with her only appearance on the BBC's 'Top Of The Pops'. It was around this period that Ambrose rejected two songs for Kathy that became massive hits for other artistes. 'You're My World', which Kathy loved, was deemed to be unsuitable and subsequently recorded by Cilla Black; likewise 'Something Is Happening' was then recorded by Herman's Hermits.

Chapter Four

You Go Your Way, I'll Go Mine

"My client does not do screen tests."

Bert Ambrose.

I

Kathy's series ended its run in the March of that year. It was due to return in the August where the shows would then be screened on every third Saturday. The ITV programmers took advantage of the singer's break in her BBC contract and she topped the bill on 'Sunday Night At The London Palladium', eighteen months after her last appearance on the top rated show. The BBC TV series now increased her theatre engagement fees to around £5,000 per week. She also sang that year on ABC's 'Eamonn Andrews Show'.

In May she flew to America to appear on Ed Sullivan's legendary television show. This was screened on May 23rd and led to many offers of work in both cabaret and television for later in the year. Unfortunately Ambrose had already fixed her summer season engagements, which began the following month, so reluctantly the lucrative offers had to be turned down. Decca had long since released her singles into the US market and, although none had charted, they all had gained considerable airplay, and so she was not an unknown quantity in the USA.

Because of the BBC commitments, a long summer season was out of the question, so Kathy accepted billing as 'special guest star' for the first six weeks of 'The Russ Conway Show', at the Winter Gardens, Bournemouth, opening on June 5th. Dusty Springfield would take over for a further six weeks from July 19th and Adele Leigh would complete the season. The box office sales dropped when Kathy left the production.

The same month Kathy opened her six-week season, Decca released her latest single, the beautiful ballad 'The Way Of Love'. However, it was almost never released. When she turned up at the Decca studios to record the number she could not sing a note. A painful nodule had developed on her vocal chords and she had lost her voice. A doctor was summoned to treat her, and it was only then, when the session was nearing its end of allotted time, that her voice began to come back. The orchestra was hurriedly recalled and within minutes the recording was completed, as within minutes her voice began to falter again. Reviewing the completed recording the Melody Maker wrote 'she really pours her heart into the plaintive lyrics. It is a superb performance and an object lesson in interpretation for any would-be singer.'

II

Kathy duly completed her autumn season for the BBC and in the December released what is undoubtedly her finest recording; the album 'Make Someone Happy – My Heart Sings'. The LP remains in the memory today for having the strange distinction of not mentioning Kathy by name either on the front or back cover. However, in 1965, with a large colour photograph of Kathy smiling straight out at the record buying public, no one needed to be told who the artiste singing on the album was.

Also that December she made headlines in the Press when she fainted while on stage during a performance at the Royal Festival Hall. Ambrose blamed the pressure of work. Days later, Kathy was very upset to discover that two of her favourite stage gowns, valued at around £600, were stolen from the car she was travelling to an engagement in.

1966 began with Kathy's completion of her contract for the BBC and Ambrose was about to commit the first of two grave errors of judgement from which her career would never really recover.

Not realising that the BBC was actively preparing future projects for their "golden girl", Ambrose signed a contract with Rediffusion for Kathy to star in her own series on the commercial channel. The agreement was for 13 weekly spectaculars to be called 'Kathy Kirby Sings'. It was to be recorded and screened in the autumn. To mark the new deal Kathy headlined another bill on ATV's Sunday Night at the London Palladium.

It was also announced that she was to star in a colour film musical, probably based on her life story. Ambrose, having had many film offers for Kathy in the last few years, had rejected them all, waiting for what he considered the right project to come along. This production would be distributed by ABC and directed by Marcel Hellman, who had recently received rave reviews for his production of 'Moll Flanders'.

The project, however, would never come to fruition. Kathy would reveal later that Ambrose did not consider that she should agree to a film test, one clause that the production company insisted upon. Another misjudgement by the former bandleader.

The New Year continued with more single releases; such as her vocal version of the instrumental hit 'Spanish Flea', and the lovely ballad 'Where in the World?'. The cabaret and concert work kept her busy along with further guest spots on Bruce Forsyth's spectacular for ITV, and a return date on 'The Eamonn Andrews Show'.

In June, Kathy and Ambrose flew to Majorca to fulfil two cabaret dates at the Club Tago Mago, before opening in her summer season at the vast Winter Gardens, Margate on July 5th 1966.

During the previous summer she had headlined Sunday concerts at the same venue, supported by Jon Pertwee and the guitarist, Bert Weedon. The management at the Winter Gardens, thrilled by the business, now invited her back to headline her own show.

'The Kathy Kirby Show' was directed and staged by Ross Taylor, with a supporting bill that included Saveen and Daisy May, the comedian Derek Dene and teenage trumpet star, Nigel Hopkins. The show broke all box office records and the Thanet headlines read, 'Kathy Kirby-Toast of Margate'

Reviewing the show, Reg Foster said: "Earlier in the production she sang 'This Is My Kind of Town' with the full company, and attired in male evening dress gave a wonderful impersonation of the late Vesta Tilley with 'The Man Who Broke The Bank at Monte Carlo'. At the end of the show the capacity audience gave her a tremendous ovation, after she had sung for forty minutes. The general verdict was that The Kathy Kirby Show was the best summer show ever to be seen in Margate. Amongst the numbers she sang in her closing spots were 'Hava Nagilah', 'Make Someone Happy, 'My Man' and 'Spanish Flea'.

Two weeks before opening in Margate Kathy appeared on June 26th as top of the bill on the second show of ITV's 'Blackpool Night Out. At the time her new recording was a double A side featuring 'Will I Ever Learn?' and 'The Adam Adamant Theme'. The latter was the title number for the popular BBC drama series starring Gerald Harper. However, although it was the theme song, Kathy could hardly sing the popular BBC number on prime time ITV, so she sang the flip side. Also on the bill were the Dallas Boys.

It is interesting that that just a few years later Kathy admitted to the Press that the ITV company presenting 'Blackpool Night

Out' had originally wanted her to host the entire series, singing a couple of numbers each week. Ambrose declined the offer and the job went to the Birmingham born comic, Tony Hancock.

Two major turning points occurred during the summer season in Margate. In the July, Kathy and Decca parted company after a contract with EMI had been negotiated. More important however was the headline that greeted Kathy and Ambrose during their stay in Margate.

'Kathy Kirby's TV series is scrapped' read the banner headlines. The Rediffusion series 'Kathy Kirby Sings' had been dropped from the autumn network schedules. The main disagreement was over how the singer should be presented to the viewers.

Ambrose had his ideas, and the company had theirs. Kathy would not be drawn into giving a statement to the Press, other than that she was "very disappointed", although she did reveal that she was "stunned" when she found that the proposed regular guest, David Jacobs, was having dancing lessons in preparation for the show!

Within six months Ambrose had taken Kathy from the BBC and now the ITV networks. It must have been of little consolation that the replacement ITV series, with Millicent Martin and David Jacobs, was far from the success hoped for. Most critics panned it, and it was soon re-scheduled out of the prime time viewing period.

Although Kathy would continue to appear on television for a few more years following Ambrose's decision, she never again had a series of her own, and her guest appearances became fewer and less frequent.

III

One Sunday, early in the Margate season, Kathy joined the cabaret cast for a Royal party at Windsor Castle. The Press duly reported how Kathy had been the success of the evening, and how thrilled the singer was when the Queen told her how much she enjoyed her spectacular shows on the small screen. The following day the singer had a general check up and was advised to take things a little easier. Unfortunately, apart from the run in Margate, she was due to begin a series of concerts at the Pavilion Theatre, Bournemouth, seven in all, from July 24th.

She had already missed a few Margate performances due to laryngitis and bronchitis, and she prepared for the concerts at Bournemouth against her doctor's wishes.

With no series to look forward to, Ambrose arranged a tour of South Africa, with Jess Conrad guesting, lasting six weeks and totting up some 20,000 miles. Both Ambrose and Kathy were heavily criticised in some sections of the Press for accepting the engagement. At around that time several thousand Equity members had signed a declaration not to appear before a colour barred audience. Kathy released a Press statement which read: "I think it is wrong for artistes to take part in politics. You cannot dictate to a government how to run its own business."

The tour would include two concerts for a black only audience, the rest were for white audiences. Opening in Johannesburg, and continuing to Cape Town and its surrounding areas, whatever the UK Press thought of it, the tour was a tremendous success.

Ambrose and Kathy returned home wondering what kind of welcome they would receive from either television channel, if any.

Chapter Five

Tom Jones, Rumours, And The Talk Of The Town

'My fans are reassured if I look the part of a star'
Kathy Kirby

I

Ironically, during the next few years, without an exclusive contract with either channel, Kathy, by concentrating on theatre, cabaret and concert work, would earn far more money doing live shows, sometimes working fifty weeks of the year.

Moving into her new £50,000 house in Mayfair, her first single on the EMI label was released. 'No One's Gonna Hurt You Any more' was the first of many records she would issue in the singles' market with this company, and although none of them charted, many contain her finest recording work. The B-side of the first single was a recording of a song that had long featured in her act, 'My Yiddishe Momma'. A superb rendition, as the reviewer for the New Musical Express noted: "This is pure quality. I think perhaps even Sophie Tucker would have approved."

Ambrose's continuous talks with the TV stations finally paid off and Kathy was soon back in the studios to record a one-off special 'Here Comes Kathy'. She chose her guests from the old days of 'Stars and Garters', with Tommy Bruce and Clinton Ford supporting her.

Her return to the television screens in her own show provided her with sixth spot in the ratings. It also came first in an identikit programme survey judges by 11 million viewers. It shouldn't have come as any surprise to the television powers. Hadn't her BBC series lifted the average figures from six million to a record breaking 18 million when she was on the screen?

Even when ITV scheduled the then highly popular series 'Burke's Law, starring Gene Barry, opposite her it made no difference. With the success of the special, a series was rumoured to be in discussion, however, nothing came of it.

Kathy's fan club was now being run by the highly efficient Mary Clarke, based in Warrington, and I duly looked forward to my newsletter each month. In April and May 1967 I caught her act again at two prestigious nightspots. On April 9th she was the very first girl singer to appear at the newly opened Batley Variety Club, which proved a tremendously successful week for her. The following month she appeared as guest star for the opening of the Cavendish Club in Sheffield, and sang before an invited audience of some 300 guests on the Thursday night, and again for the general public on the Friday.

JH

II

Her summer season was approaching, and Kathy had been

given the choice of venues. Co-starring (but with second billing) with Bruce Forsyth at the vast Opera House in Blackpool, or topping the bill at the lovely Winter Gardens. It was no surprise that Ambrose and Kathy chose the latter. 'The Kathy Kirby Show' opened on June 17th with a cast that included Donald Peers, Johnny Hackett and Jimmy Logan, who split the season with Ted Rogers.

Originally the legendary comic Freddie Frinton had been billed to appear, but had to withdraw due to ill health. Millicent Martin would join Bruce Forsyth at the Opera House for the summer season. It was not the spectacular success hoped for.

Kathy broke every box office record at the Winter Gardens that season. The first girl singer ever to have her own show in the building, and once again it was staged by the man responsible for her Margate success, Ross Taylor. In her nightly spot she included a new number in her act, the twenties torch song, 'Buddy Can You Spare a Dime?', which stopped the show every night. A little while later her fan club ran a poll to decide amongst its members which was Kathy's most popular song. Surprisingly none of her hit records made the top three. Third choice was 'Acapulco 22', second came 'Turn Around', but first came 'Buddy Can You Spare a Dime?' It was a number she was never to record, but sadly became prophetic in many ways.

Kathy's arrangement with theatre engagements in the sixties was usually for a fixed fee, together with an agreed percentage of the box office takings.

This percentage usually worked out at around £10,000 in cash to be paid out by the box office on a Saturday evening. The money was usually collected by Ambrose, generally to be spent (and normally lost) in the nearest casino that same night.

Following her completion of the Blackpool season, she made her first appearance on the BBC since turning her back on them. Although BBC2 still only had a small share of the audience in those days, she topped the bill on 'International Cabaret', introduced by Kenneth Williams, and filmed from London's most famous nightspot, The Talk Of The Town.

On Saturday October 28th 1967 she finally returned to her old BBC studios to face a much wider audience for 'The Val Doonican Show'. As the special guest, she sang a couple of numbers and shared a duet with the star.

Another appearance for the BBC was on November 11th when she sang on Simon Dee's chat show 'Dee Time', and for a while it looked as if, maybe, the corporation had forgiven their 'Golden Girl' for walking out on them.

On November 2nd 1967 Kathy began a three-week tour with Tom Jones and the Ted Heath Band, playing 20 different venues on the tour. Staged by Gordon Mills, the Ted Heath Band, then celebrating the 21st anniversary of their formation, would back Kathy's performance, which occupied the entire first half, and

Tom Jones the second.

Although the two singers had shared the Decca label for a while, they hardly knew each other well. He had guested on one of her BBC shows, and during the Blackpool summer season, Jones had appeared in a Sunday concert at her theatre. However, not long after the tour was completed the rumours started about the two stars that have continued to this day.

The tour proved to be an enormous success for both artistes. Some thought Kathy was crazy for accepting the engagement. Surely the screaming girl fans of the country's top sex idol would hardly be her ideal audience. The sceptics could not have been more wrong. From Glasgow to Bournemouth, she was a success, indeed, in Edinburgh, the audience simply would not let her leave the stage.

III

Her next single, 'Turn Around', was released on November 17th 1967. The previous effort, 'In All The World', failed to get anywhere at all.

She appeared on ATV's 'The Golden Shot', to plug the single, guesting with Eddie Calvert. Now, no longer with Decca, the recording company was quick to release a compilation long player of her work for them. Entitled 'The Best of Kathy Kirby', sales were good, so another under the title of 'The World of Kathy Kirby' soon followed.

1968 began with Kathy continuing the round of Britain's booming nightclub circuit. In the first month of the year she played the Fiesta Club in Stockton on Tees, followed by the Piccadilly Club in Glasgow and Caesar's Palace, Luton.

Scottish TV televised the singer in a programme recorded at the Piccadilly Club, and with its success the papers reported that the company wanted Kathy to appear in a series for them. However, nothing materialised. Around the same time another Press report announced that the BBC had signed her for six half hour programmes, but once again nothing came of it

Kathy did star in a one-of special for BBC2, simply called 'Kate', as part of the 'Something Special' series. The cast was all female and included special guests Libby Morris and the all girl orchestra led by Betty Smith. The programme revived the memories of the 'Stars and Garters' days, with a pub setting where the invited audience turned out to be a collection of off-duty London policemen!

IV

On Easter Monday Kathy achieved one of her lifelong ambitions, by staring at London's most famous nightspot, The Talk of The Town. The season would run for a month until May 11th. At the request of the club directors she wore her hair swept high on her head, rejecting her usual curly, bouncy style. The season was a considerable success for her, and Ambrose would proudly tell the Press at the end of the engagement that the theatre management rated Kathy as one of the top four artistes, British or otherwise, to have played the Talk of The Town during the past ten years.

It was just a couple of weeks later that Kathy would break down on stage, while performing the same act at the La Dolce Vita nightclub in Birmingham. A poison pen campaign came to a climax while the singer was appearing in cabaret at the venue. As Ambrose told the Press: "It is a most insidious campaign with letters, whispers and telephone calls coming in from all over the country. I have now consulted my solicitor as Kathy's health is being ruined by it all."

The worst letters had been posted from Stratford-upon-Avon and Walsall, and at one point during the Birmingham engagement, Kathy was so upset she was scared to go on stage.

On the opening night a drunk in the audience had shouted out, enquiring how 'Tom Jones' bastard child was?' - Kathy, too stunned to answer, moved quickly on. The following evening, however, after receiving more letters asking her how she felt it necessary to 'steal other people's husbands to produce her own little bastards', just proved too much for her. Faltering as she sang 'Someone to Watch Over Me', she broke down and ran from the stage. She returned to complete her performance, simply saying that she had received a rather unpleasant note which had upset her. She had finally come face to face with the wicked rumour that had been haunting her for the past eighteen months.

V

After a short rest, she continued with the club engagements, earning around £2,000 a week. Capacity audiences were reported at the Spennymoor Variety Club, the Cavendish in Blackburn, and there was a return to Birmingham, appearing at the lavish Castaway. A week that went by without incident.

A new single hit the record shops, 'I Almost Called Your Name', and on July 7th Kathy starred in 'The Big Show' for ITV.

Her new album was in the shops and the title track was the song she would choose to close her performances from then on, 'My Thanks To You'. One reviewer noted at the time: "It may be a long time since Kathy Kirby had a disc in the top ten, but 'My Thanks To You' shows she is still one of the most devastating singers around."

The album was, and is, a showcase for Kathy's vocal ability. A collection of oldies and more recent numbers. Stand out tracks included the title song 'If I Loved You' and 'It Only Happens When I Dance With You'.

Deciding against appearing in a long summer season that year, in addition to her nightclub work, Kathy undertook a series of Sunday concerts around the major seaside holiday towns, including Douglas, on the Isle of Man, Torquay, Great Yarmouth and a return visit to Blackpool.

A dahlia was named after her, and a fascinating double page spread in the Sunday Mirror devoted itself to a meeting the singer had with the leading fashion designer, Mary Quant.

This meeting took place because Kathy thought about trying a new image to get away from the glamorous figure hugging Kirby gowns, blonde curls and sophisticated look. She asked for a meeting with Miss Quant to see what the innovative designer suggested. Kathy, then 28, had always dressed in a manner far older than her years when appearing on stage or television. Mary was about to rectify this.

With dresses from her Ginger Group collection out went the revealing, beaded gowns, to be replaced by feminine, cotton, 'girl next door' number. The Kirby hair was pulled right back from the forehead and ringlets fell loosely either side of the face. With Kathy's own peaches and cream complexion the years just fell away, and the Kirby glamour girl had disappeared. In her place was someone who looked suspiciously like her daughter.

Kathy loved the look, but ever the show business realist noted: "No matter what I think I doubt my audiences will like it. There is a sort of tradition about stage dresses and how I am expected to look."

She knew what her fans expected only too well. A poll run by Mark Clarke, the secretary of her fan club, was held soon after the Sunday Mirror article. The new look was rejected by the majority of her fan club members.

My close friend, Eric Latimer, was the stage manager for a host of stars during the late sixties at the Castaway Club in Birmingham, and I asked him if he had any recollections of his time there, and of Kathy in particular.

He writes:-

The club was probably the most impressive nightclub in Europe at that time, and every Sunday afternoon world famous stars would arrived for their band call. Some are still at the top of the show business ladder, (such as Tom Jones and Englebert), and others have faded from view. A great number too have passed on, such as Frankie Howerd, Dickie Valentine, Tommy Cooper and Tommy Trinder.

As Stage Manager I would I would check with each artiste, or their personal assistant, just what was required by way of lighting, and would explain the set up, dressing rooms, microphone layout, and apologise for the always problematic sound system. The room itself was artistically done with palm trees, a beached schooner, a couple of log cabins, and the rest, so the sound 'bounce' was always a huge problem. The installation itself was inadequate, having been put in by a telephone company rather than professionals in the field. In short, a nightmare for those performing and a worse one for the sound operator behind the stick. It was always 'no lay-back, too much feedback'.

Kathy Kirby arrived, with much interest in her since the recent wrangles with the TV companies had made headline news. Some newspaper articles had been unkind, labelling her 'difficult' to work with, and I wondered about the truth of it all. Certainly she was the object of many gazes and much interest.

However, there is no doubt about it, she performed excellently, and audiences were enraptured by her every performance. I used to govern events from the side of the stage, and, of course watched every performer. I remember admiring her work and applauding every time, and musing how sweet she looked in the lights which showed up her blonde tresses, and how the light played through the pink beads hanging on the sleeves of her lurex dress.

There was a slight problem on the first night; there usually was until the show had run in a little. Kathy complained that the microphones were, "making her sound scratch, like Cilla Black." Adjustments to the bass knob were made and her mother, always floating around the room during her daughter's spot, passed by the sound corner and said: "That was much better, the sound is OK now."

Kathy was not so readily satisfied and demanded more

attention to the system. I said that according to her mother, who had checked every inch of the room, everything was fine. Miss Kirby told me in no uncertain terms that her mother was not to be listened to. Eventually the right notches were found and the week continued successfully and happily.

The shows at The Castaway were 'scratch' variety shows, which meant that each week a collection of different artistes were assembled in the running order/programme, as is different from a company which stays together on tour, presenting the same show all the time. The dancers, the Ballet Montmartre, however, were regular performers.

The club director, Mr John Reeve, wanted some form of production in the show, rather than the continuous presentation of individual variety acts, to make it more of a complete production. He asked me to arrange something for the week Kathy Kirby was appearing. I thought it would be ideal to have all the artistes walk down at the end of the evening's entertainment, rather like a pantomime finale walk down, as a final goodnight gesture.

Miss Kirby was outraged and said I should contact her agent, and that it was not in her contract, and it made the whole thing 'like a show'.

I pointed out as delicately as I could that this was precisely what we needed and it was exactly what the audience would *appreciate. Kathy, however, would have none of it. She did her act and was not in 'a show'*

The story of the backstage at the Castaway is a long and tempestuous one. Some artistes were 'trouble'; others were charming and surprisingly friendly. Kathy's week was quite professional and uneventful as far as I was concerned. There were many artistes following, quite big names even today, who would have done well to give us just half of the power and dynamism tat Kathy Kirby showed that week. Her power and projection were second to none, and she could almost have performed without the 'Cilla Black' microphones!

Chapter Six

Miss Kirby Regrets

"I'm vain enough to hate it when fans ask me why I don't appear as often as I used to on television. I have to say it's because I'm not wanted."

Kathy Kirby.

I

Following the Mary Quant article the Daily Mail ran a large piece on Kathy, highlighting the fact that a great number of readers had been writing to the paper's Press office inquiring why Kathy was not appearing on television as she used to. True, she didn't dominate both channels with her own shows, however, guest spots still continued to be offered, and on stage she was still big box office. The article hinted that Ambrose was currently having talks with the new Thames Television Company for Kathy to return to the small screen for them in her own series. This negotiation, yet again, came to nothing.

Kathy's next television appearance should have been screened on August 17th, as the special guest star on the 'Van Johnson Show'. Although recorded, it was never shown due to the ITV strike at the time. However, she did appear in another television show from the London Palladium. As with 'Van Johnson' it was made with a view to the American market, and the Palladium shows in the series had a major US name featured each week. The edition Kathy appeared in officially starred Lorne Green, from the hit western, 'Bonanza', with a special guest appearance by Roger Moore. The two stars, however, did little more than linking spots between acts, and the real variety was provided by Kathy, Millicent Martin, the late Tommy Cooper and Roy Castle. It was Kathy who had the most screen time, singing four numbers in all.

The autumn continued with cabaret and a two-week theatre engagement of 'The Kathy Kirby Show' in Bournemouth and Wolverhampton. The supporting company included Solomon King, then riding high with his hit record, 'She Wears My Ring' and Daley and Wayne, the well-known club act. The review in the Wolverhampton Express and Star read, 'The vivacious singer takes the house by storm as variety returns to the Grand Theatre after an eight month absence. The blonde bombshell of a girl has both personality and the voice to set the seal on any production. Kathy Kirby brings warmth, humour and pathos to her singing, which includes many of the songs that have made her famous.'

She rounded off the year with a week at the Theatre Club in Wakefield, opening on December 15th. A new record was released, a double A side consisting of 'Antonio' and 'Come Back Here With My Heart'. Television appearances to plug the recording came in, and she sang 'Antonio' on 'Frost of Sunday', 'The Jimmy Tarbuck Show' and 'Will The Real Mike Yarwood Stand Up?' In the Tarbuck show she also appeared with the comic in a sketch, and for Mike Yarwood, appeared as Vicky Carby'. (Vicki Carr) sending up the American vocalist with her hit number 'It Must Be Him'. Kathy also sang 'Come Back Here With My Heart' on a live edition of 'The Golden Shot', with Bob Monkhouse. The programme is remembered today for the vast amount of technical hitches that took place. With time running out, it was a small miracle that Kathy had time to appear at the end of the programme at all. It was only due to Monkhouse's supreme professionalism that the programme survived its Sunday afternoon slot on that particular occasion.

Kathy also topped the bill on ATV's 'Saturday Variety' show on December 14th. Singing both sides of her new record and the number 'I'll Always Love You So', it looked as though her return to television on a regular basis was about to happen, for it had been some time since she had been on the small screen so often.

II

Kathy opened 1969 with a terrific success at the Fiesta Club in Stockton, and became the first girl singer to headline at the Pocco Club in Stockport. The review of the Stockport engagement in the Stage tells it as it was. 'On the night I paid a visit, the star attraction was Kathy Kirby, who, from the moment she came on the cabaret floor, made a colossal impact. She had the audience in the palm of her hand throughout her fifty minute spot, holding them all spell-bound with a performance of outstanding quality, diction, appearance and microphone technique.'

Television appearances followed in Holland and Portugal, but announced guest spots over here in 'The Ronnie Corbett Follies Show' and 'The Vicki Carr Show' did not happen. Her new record was called 'I'll Catch The Sun', released on March 21st. Written by Rod McKuen, it was the title song from the film 'Joanna'. The day following the release of the single, Kathy flew with Ambrose to Australia for cabaret engagements at both the Chevron Hilton and Chequers, at a reported £18,000 for the five-week tour. She also undertook a number of television appearances whilst over there, and flew back to England well pleased with her work, which had gathered standing ovations most nights.

Following a holiday, Kathy now prepared for her first summer season in two years. The Festival Hall in Paignton had opened the previous year with the then record breaking 'Black and White Minstrel Show' in residence. This year the choice was Kathy Kirby starring in Gerald Palmer's lavish summer spectacular 'Up and Away', presented by Tom Arnold. Opening on June 7th, it would run through until the end of September. Second billed was Billy Dainty then fresh from his success in BBC Television's

'Kindly Leave The Stage' series, and Len Lowe; also a second appearance in a Kirby show summer season by the teenage trumpet star, Nigel Hopkins.

By now I had lost track of all the times I had seen Kathy work. I remember my particular visit to Paignton extremely well though. I travelled down for a week's holiday during my summer school break with a close friend, Jasbir Singh. I had booked for the two of us to catch three performances. Jasbir was far from impressed, thinking her old fashioned in both her style and her dress. Unlike previous summer appearances, Kathy elected not to appear throughout the show, making her only entrance towards the end of the second half for her 'top of the bill' spot. Naturally she went as well as ever, but she was fortunate in having someone with the comic genius of the late Billy Dainty to keep the rest of the production moving.

JH

III

Just before opening in Paignton, Weston Taylor interviewed Kathy for an article in the News Of The World. The headline said it all, 'I've Been Silly'. She explained just why she hadn't been appearing on television as much as she used to.

"I've something to confess. I've been a really silly, naughty girl with the television people over here. That's why I've not been seen on the screen in my own show for ages," she said.

Explaining why she left the BBC and not realising the corporation had other projects in mind for her, and her disappointment when she withdrew from the Rediffusion series she had signed for. She continued, "the shape of the programme was different from what I'd understood had been arranged. I felt it would do me more harm than good. Within two months I'd left both the BBC and ITV without realising the sort of harm it would cause me in all sorts of ways."

Kathy also discussed the problems she had encountered at her recent visit to La Dolce Vita nightclub in Birmingham and the hate mail she had received. She told Taylor that as soon as she first heard of the stories of her supposed affair with Tom Jones, she telephoned the star's wife to explain it was all lies and pass on a message of sympathy. She went on to say that with being off-screen so much recently, she had lost count of the rumours and the places where she was supposed to have had their baby. She added that during her recent Australian tour, the pop idol had also been out there. They didn't see each other, but spoke briefly on the telephone. In fact she hadn't actually seen him since their major concert engagement two years previously.

On completion of the Paignton season, Kathy released her cover version of Peggy Lee's hit, 'Is That All There Is?'

IV

Now averaging around £60,000 a year, Kathy would open 1970 by making special changes in her business life. Although Ambrose would continue to be by her side, he wasn't now in the best of health and so her co-manager became Bill Preston. She also returned to the agency she had broken with the year before. It was run by Michael Grade, son of Leslie Grade, who had helped to found one of Europe's greatest theatrical agencies, London Management.

With another new record about to be released, which she would sing on ITV's 'Mike & Bernie Winters Show', articles appeared in the Daily and Sunday newspapers with headlines such as 'It's Golden Girl Again', and 'On Her Way Back', 'The Girl Who Walked Out On The Box'. In one piece, discussing her past disputes with the various TV companies, she admitted that she had probably made more money since leaving television, but that it was 'a matter of pride'. She also revealed that she had never considered appearing in pantomime, as the pay wasn't enough.

To coincide with her return to ITV, the TV Times ran a three-page colour spread on Kathy, welcoming her back. The song she sang on the 'Winters Show' was her cover version of the old Kay Starr number, 'Wheel Of Fortune'. Although given an updated treatment and a great performance by Kathy, the song was hopelessly dated and was quickly forgotten.

Then living in a plush flat in London's Grosvenor Square, Kathy at 29, and very few unpublished romances behind her, was persuaded to go on a blind date by close friends. The date in question turned out to be a wealthy Leeds based hosiery distributor called Geoffrey Gee, who was 34. The first evening the two of them went to see Caterina Valente in cabaret, and at supper afterwards talked long into the early hours. Very soon Gee would become the most important man in her life; after Ambrose.

When appearing at such nightspots as the Whitcombe Lodge in Gloucestershire, Kathy would soon start telling her audience of Gee's existence. "I mustn't be too long out here," she confided, "last night Geoffrey went off without me." They became very close during the early months of 1970, and the Leeds millionaire showered Kathy with gifts; a racehorse, a Yorkshire terrier called Geeki, who Kathy would totally adore, a Meissen vase, which Geeki would break, and a converted luxury house in Leeds where Kathy would come to spend some considerable time. The dog, incidentally, was the proud owner of his own gilt-edged kennel.

Geoffrey would visit Kathy wherever she was appearing and the newspapers rumoured that an engagement ring would soon be sparkling on the hand of Britain's best known bachelor show girl.

V

That summer she appeared in her last top flight summer

production. Presented by Bernard Belfont, at the Theatre Royal, Brighton, Kathy top billed in a production called, 'Startime'. Also starring was Arthur Askey and a guest appearance by the legendary music hall star, Miss Hetty King. The bill also had Saveen and Daisy May, the male vocalist Heathmore, TV's Go Jos and a virtually unknown comedian who brought the house down every night, Larry Grayson.

I travelled to Brighton by train with my Grandfather to see the show. Arriving back in London from the coast, we found that we had missed the last train back to Birmingham. My grandfather, then retired and myself, in my last year at school, found funds notwithstanding, had little choice but to sleep on Euston Station until the first milk train left in the early hours of the next morning. We arrived home shattered, but for me, as ever, seeing Kathy made it worth it.

JH

Kathy had long relied on the advice given to her by the fortune-teller, Eva Petulengro. One night during her run at Brighton, Kathy was visited by Miss Petulengro, she received the news that she has never, not even to this day, recovered from. The fortune-teller predicted that within twelve months Ambrose would be dead, he had seven or eight months at the most. Kathy was devastated. The man was her entire life. He was her manager, her mentor, the father she never had and also, in the end, the one great love of her life.

Soon after the Brighton season finished, Kathy made headlines again, after being admitted to St. George's Hospital in south London after a suspected drug overdose. It was dismissed as an accident, but one can only wonder at the strain Kathy, who was naturally highly emotional, was now under that September. Ambrose had recently suffered a mild stroke and without any publicity had been secretly admitted to a London clinic. After treatment Kathy took him to Barbados to recuperate. Gradually the former bandleader recovered, and the hugely relieved singer must have thought that for once Eva Petulengro must have been wrong.

Returning home, Kathy rounded off the year by singing her newest single on ITV's 'Leslie Crowther' series. Filmed at the Palace Theatre 'My Way' had of course become a hit for Frank Sinatra and Dorothy Squires. However, Kathy closely identified with the lyrics, and finding her stage audiences liked her interpretation, expressed a desire to put it down on vinyl.

The months went by with Ambrose now looking and feeling much better. Kathy was still involved with Geoffrey Gee, and busy on the cabaret circuit. In June she travelled to Leeds to record a guest appearance on Les Dawson's new Yorkshire TV series 'Sez Lez'. She would never recover from the events of that day in the television studios.

Chapter Seven

When Day Is Done

"He developed me as a person. He meant everything to me. I'll never get over his death.

Kathy Kirby.

I

On the bill of 'Sez Lez', in which Kathy was to be the chief guest star, singing with the resident band of Syd Lawrence, were Alan Price, Georgie Fame and John Cleese. Arriving at her dressing room she noticed some plastic flowers. Kathy was horrified. An old show business tradition meant that they would bring bad luck. Ambrose immediately threw them out, but Kathy was still unsettled as she mounted the huge staircase on which she would sing her number 'Come Rain, Come Shine', surrounded by the gentlemen of the orchestra.

Waiting for Les Dawson to introduce her, she saw from the corner of her eye the show's producer gently approach her. Ambrose had, moments before, been taken ill in her dressing room. Dashing from the set she found him collapsed on the floor screaming in pain. Immediately transferred to the Leeds General Infirmary, she stayed with him until he seemed calmer and in slightly less pain. The old bandleader, ever the decision maker, told Kathy to get back to the studio and record her spot. Knowing, as ever, she had no choice when it came to arguing with Ambrose, she reluctantly agreed. At the studio Syd Lawrence, who had worked with Ambrose in the old days, took Kathy on one side just before the camera rolled. 'Make this one for Bert,' he said.

On that staircase she sang 'Come Rain, Come Shine', as she had never sung it before. She was sensational. She would also never sing the song again.

Kathy returned immediately to the hospital to learn that Ambrose needed an emergency operation if there was any chance of him surviving. The singer was horrified, knowing that major surgery for anyone of his age was a risk. Terrified, she went to see him in his private room. "Did you do the song?" were the first words that greeted her. Reassuring him that she had and it had gone well, Kathy saw her mentor lifted onto a trolley to be taken down to theatre. Holding his hand she walked the short distance to the lift before leaving him to face what would be a six-hour operation. The last words Ambrose spoke to Kathy before the lift doors closed was typical of the man, "Get back to London and get your rest". Reminding her that she opened in cabaret the following Sunday in Caerphilly, the singer attempted to argue the point. His parting shot was a smile and the words "do as I say, I'm your manager, I know best."

Geoffrey Gee arrived at the hospital and they returned to his house to wait for news on the six-hour operation. Entering the house in Leeds, the telephone was ringing. Ambrose had died ten minutes after Kathy had kissed him goodbye.

It was in a state of shock and disbelief that Kathy arranged the funeral of her manager. Although a Catholic girl, she organised the Jewish service for Ambrose. The chief mourner, she scattered the first handful of clay on the coffin. The singer had never been to a funeral before.

With Ambrose gone, Kathy would move constantly from one agent and manager to another, never finding what she was looking for. With the constant changes, came the headlines too, in the end leaving a scar over her career and a feeling of frustration for her fans that her career was being wasted.

She went into mourning and cancelled all her immediate cabaret work. Eventually she gave a Press interview, on the eve of a new record release, and a return to the cabaret circuit. She finally admitted what many in show business already knew. "I was in love with him more than I can ever tell you. It's time the world knew, he was the only reason I did not marry anyone else." She spoke publicly for the first time, of how they had indeed discussed marriage, but Ambrose, in the end, would rule it out due to the massive difference in their ages. He believed it might harm her career. Still numb with grief she spoke of how he had made every decision for her, and now with his death she had been searching for a letter he might have left for her, advising her what to do now.

Still seeing Geoffrey Gee, although she couldn't possibly think of marriage to anyone else at that moment, she finally returned to work, making an appearance in cabaret at a country club in Weston Super Mare. Wearing Bert's favourite white stage gown, Kathy sang just one number in his memory, his old signature tune, 'When Day Is Done'. The lyrics could not have been more appropriate. She also sang her new release 'So Here I Go Again'.

II

In the seventies the South Pier Theatre, Blackpool had the reputation of having summer shows that weren't quite up to the standard and class of the town's Winter Gardens, Opera House and North Pier Theatre. This was to be the venue of Kathy's 1971, and indeed last, summer season to date. It was also the turning point in the singer's career, for Kathy was not top of the bill for the first time in many a year. Sharing the spot for 'The Big Show of 1971' was Harry H. Corbett, of Steptoe fame, his name over the title on the left hand side, and on the right came Kathy's name. Technically second billed. Also featured were Dave Dee, without Dozy, Beaky, Mick and Titch, and the ex-Rocking Berries vocalist, Clive Lea.

As ever I travelled over to see the show. Again with my old friend Jasbir, we stayed for a long weekend in Blackpool, and I knew only too well it was Blackpool he wanted to explore and not the opportunity to see Kathy. The show wasn't a particularly good one, Harry H. Corbett wasn't really summer show material. As Kathy said herself, "when he was out there dying I used to bring in the downstage cloth just to get him off, so at least I could get on with my act; how was I supposed to follow him when he's just lost the audience?" It was at this point in her career that she sang 'Without A Song' as her opening number, something she would continue to do as long as she performed.   *JH*

It was during the Blackpool run that Kathy and her manager Bill Preston clashed. Cutting his wages by 50% during the season, leaving him just £30 per week. (he would eventually take her to court for wrongful dismissal when he refused the pay cut).

The season was not a happy one for Kathy. Still in shock from the death of Ambrose, she didn't get on well with Corbett and resented being second billed, and also must have wondered how, in just four short years from playing the prestigious Winter Gardens with her own show, she was now appearing in a theatre which always had a reputation for being something of a white elephant.

Following the season she continued in cabaret, playing smaller and smaller venues, which meant that her fees were becoming smaller too. By Christmas her relationship with Geoffrey Gee was all but over, and in the New Year she made headlines again by announcing that she had fallen in love with a doctor. Said Kathy at the time: "He has a divorce pending at the moment, so I don't want to give you a name". The doctor in question was Harley Street based, Peter Stephen, who Kathy had first met when she was seeking treatment for a sore throat. Within six months their relationship would be over. During the interview Kathy mentioned that Geoffrey Gee had, in fact, asked her to marry him no less than five times during their two years together, the last time being just prior to Christmas. Newspaper reports the following day had Gee strongly denying that he had ever proposed to Kathy at any point during their friendship. During the run at Blackpool, Kathy had signed with Harry Dawson of the Mary Arnold Agency, but it wasn't to last so she asked Byron Godfrey, a 34-year-old Welshman, who claimed to have discovered Tom Jones, to look after her career. Launching their partnership, Kathy gave a series of Press interviews where the headline screamed 'I have allowed my emotions and personal life to cut across my work, but it must not happen again. I've decided to concentrate in getting my career back into top shape. I know it's taking a plunge and I've got to do something about it".

On the cabaret circuit in 1972 she played such places as the Warren Country Club, Stockport, the Maghull Country club in Liverpool, The Kingsland Restaurant in Birkenhead and the

Kingsway Casino, Southport. She recorded another single for Columbia 'Do You Really Have A Heart' and was invited to sing once more on 'The Golden Shot'. Then on tour in Scotland she chartered a plane to get her to the ATV Studios in Birmingham for the live performance, and then straight back to Scotland for her evening performance. The cost of flying would more than eat into her television fee, but it was worth it to get back on the screen again. Unfortunately bad luck seemed to dog her again, she lost her voice for a few seconds whilst singing her number, hardly helping her television comeback plans.

Publicising her appearance on 'The Golden Shot', she disclosed to journalists that she had earlier signed for 'Stars On Sunday', the Yorkshire Television programme, hosted by Jess Yates. It broadcasted on a Sunday evening and attracted millions of viewers with its line-up of stars. Unfortunately it was filmed in the same studios where Ambrose had collapsed. Facing the camera that day Kathy opened her mouth to sing and absolutely nothing came out. She tried and tried again, but terrified, she realised that it was hopeless, she would never be able to sing in that studio again.

III

1973 saw Kathy continuing in the smaller cabaret rooms around the country. It was hardly what she was used to playing, but at least she was working and still proving to be a draw.

I caught her act at The Bedford Theatre Club, which she played for a week from the 18th February, and also The Ross Sports Centre, Ross-on-Wye, which she played for three days. Other dates included the St. Helen's Rugby League Club where she was supported by the Dallas Boys, and then Pembroke Hall in Worsley, Manchester.

JH

The intervals between engagements started to stretch out more and more. She worked for just one week in May, at the Ringer Hotel near Crawley, and had only one further week the following July booked into the diary, at Stroods Hotel near Gatwick.

Kathy jumped at the chance, therefore, at a five-day tour of Scottish dates in the July. Accepting the short tour proved to be a big mistake and a personal nightmare. The tour would splash across the front pages of most newspapers, giving her headlines she could well do without. The five-date engagement was cancelled after the first two shows, the tabloids said it all 'My Week Of Hell' by Kathy Kirby, 'My Life In Ruins' and 'I Need A Miracle To Save My Career Says Kathy'.

Always the perfectionist, she never coped well with the irritation of a faulty sound system, or an under-rehearsed band. She had after all experienced the best, perhaps too soon in life. The venues on the Scottish tour were hardly number one dates and on the opening night at Dunoon two hundred of the eight hundred in the audience walked out in disgust, because the sound system was so bad she could not be heard properly. Kathy herself suggested that the audience should request their money back. It didn't help matters that the spotlight, being operated by Kathy's mother, Eileen, consistently failed to pick up the singer on stage. Worse was to come however. The singer arrived late for her next appearance at the Castle Vaults Club in Kilbirnie, having been treated by a doctor for a sore throat. The club was tiny, crowded and had no stage. During her act Kathy had yet more problems with the microphone and Eileen dashed down to the area where Kathy was attempting to work and stopped the show; calling her daughter little more than a pub singer and tramp. Kathy eventually finished her act, but more trouble followed at a party. Some policemen were heard criticising Kathy's performance. Eileen was furious. She might be able to say what she liked, but how dare anyone else? A fight developed and Kathy's mother was arrested for causing a breach of the peace. She appeared in court the following day. The case eventually went before magistrates on August 8th and Eileen was fined £5.

Meanwhile Kathy was left to ponder her career. "My future is in the hands of the gods. It will be a miracle if I ever get the chance to sing again. I have become trouble with a capital T. What agent or producer is going to book me after this?" she told the Press.

IV

Ironically, the publicity brought a flood of sympathy for the blonde star. Having thought that she had become a 'bit old hat' she had seriously considered moving to America to look for work.

She found herself inundated with showers of goodwill messages and telegrams, all begging her not to go. More importantly however, were the offers of work. These included a fifteen-minute interview and singing spot on prime time TV, a new record deal, a club tour, and several big money 'life story' newspaper contracts.

The journalist Lynda Lee Potter wrote a lovely piece on Kathy in her Daily Mail column, under the headline, 'Fight On Kathy'. It read, 'come on Kathy Kirby love. Grit your teeth, clench your fists and get back the battling spirit that made you jump up and sing at the dance hall in Ilford when you were a buxom 13. You're not the sort of lily livered lady who lies back clutching her fevered forehead saying, "I can't cope". I think you're smashing. I'd pay to come and listen to you any old day.'

Kathy did indeed pick herself up and begin again. The first engagement after Scotland was a one-night stand at the Pier Theatre in Cleethorpes. Judith Simons writing in the Daily Express took up the story. 'She stood on stage, a dainty figure, vulnerable with blonde curls, bright lipstick and a peaches and cream skin, and 16 years of exposure in the spotlight. They had never seen a performance like it in Cleethorpes, and at the end came a standing ovation with shouts of 'Keep going Kathy' Kathy, you're still the tops'. I remember myself what she said at the end of her act that night. "I feel like a rider getting back onto a horse after falling off".

The following Sunday she had a much bigger audience. Singing and talking about her recent troubles on ITV's 'Russell Harty Show', she spoke of her problems on stage and the vacuum in her life since the death of Ambrose. The following day in the Press the reviews were both kind and sympathetic. Kathy also sang her biggest hit on the show, 'Secret Love'. This time, however, unlike the recording, as half ballad and half up-tempo. The other guest that night was Jessie Mathews. Having experienced many highs and lows during her wonderful career, one can only speculate what must have been going through Miss Mathews' mind, seeing Kathy discuss her recent nightmare. Less than ten years earlier Jessie had been a guest on one of Kathy's glittering BBC shows.

V

Meanwhile an old friend was about to offer a helping hand once more. Lena Davis had written a song for Kathy as a tribute to her relationship with Bert Ambrose.

Kathy was currently without a recording contract. Her last single for EMI had been released the previous January and was called 'Little Song For You'. Although it received some airplay and she plugged it on the BBC's 'Pebble Mill At One', sales were not good, and soon after Kathy and her recording company Columbia went their separate ways. Much better was the B-side of the record, Kathy's version of the Lennon and McCartney song 'Here, There and Everywhere'. Paul McCartney would state in years to come that Kathy's rendition of his song was one of his favourite versions of the much recorded number. Incidentally, while staying in Birmingham to record Pebble Mill, Kathy made the local Press when she accidentally set fire to some rubbish in her hotel room and the fire brigade were called out.

Lena's song 'Singer With the Band' was released by the little known Orange label on November 30th. Unlike anything Kathy had ever recorded before, it caused quite a lot of interest. Up-tempo with a blues feel to it, Kathy even found herself being played on Radio One, and that hadn't happened in years. Tony Blackburn made it his record of the week. Although, in the end it failed to make the charts, it sold considerably better than her last few records, and proved what great shape her voice was still in.

Before the end of the year Kathy sold her life story to the News Of The World. The series of articles came out over a four-week period and were worth a good deal of money to her. However, for the price she was being paid the paper expected some revelations. She did not disappoint them.

She spoke publicly for the first time of how she and Ambrose became lovers when she was not quite eighteen. Of how, during their relationship, besides his obsession with making her a star, he totally dominated her every thought and movement. Virtually a prisoner in her own Grosvenor Square mansion, he decided who she would see and not see, denying her virtually any close relationship with anyone her own age, who she might become attracted to. Deciding what songs she would sing, how she would perform them and how to dress and make up. He controlled her mind, protecting and possessing her completely. After every show he would take her back to their mansion and see that she was settled for the night before going out on the town, in London's West End, to gamble until the early hours of the morning. His gambling habits had long become legendary in London, but it wasn't until his death that Kathy discovered he had stolen from her, forging her name on cheques to feed his habit.

Kathy also revealed how, at the height of her fame in the mid-sixties, she had fallen totally in love with the entertainer Bruce Forsyth. An appearance together in cabaret at the Savoy Hotel had initially brought the two of them together. Obviously attracted to each other, Kathy admitted that had Forsyth proposed marriage she would have readily accepted. Ambrose was both jealous and furious about the friendship, and did all he could to stop the two of them seeing each other. So much so that in the end they had to meet in secret. Finally Ambrose demanded Kathy should never see him again. Although Kathy loved Bruce deeply, how could she refuse Ambrose? The singer had so much to thank her mentor for and she knew by rejecting him it would destroy him, as by this time he was living totally for her.

She also spoke of Tom Jones for the first time, and the smear campaign that had caused her such heartache. She was convinced the rumours and gossip were spread by some jealous rival who wished to destroy her career, and not by some deranged mind; something she believes to this day.

Chapter Eight

Marriage, And Rings On Her Fingers

"People may think of me as a stabber. But he was hitting me. I just picked up the knife."

Kathy Kirby

I

Before the end of 1973 Kathy would yet again make the news with problems in her personal life. Soon after returning from a major concert in Israel the police were called to her West End flat to find Byron Godfrey clutching an arm wound made by a knife. He was taken to the casualty department of St. George's Hospital, where he had five stitches in the wound. As he refused to make a formal complaint to the police an officer announced that the incident 'was of a domestic nature and no further action would be taken'. It did lead to more headlines, which Kathy could well have done without.

The singer was forced to arrange a Press conference, and sporting a sleeveless gown, which exposed a large bruise on her left arm, told the media how she feared the knife row could ruin her future. "I've been getting lots of offers of work, but they'll probably cancel after this." The fight between Kathy and Godfrey was the result of a heated exchange over the singer's high expenses. It was the beginning of the end for the two of them, and Godfrey would soon move out of the picture.

Kathy then signed with Sydney Rose, but the working relationship lasted for just a little longer than it took for the ink to dry on the contract. A small piece appeared in the popular Press about her, when she found a treasured ring given to her by Ambrose was missing from her bedside drawer. Soon after dialling 999, before they had time to arrive, she found the piece, one of many incidents attracting huge amounts of publicity that would surround her and her jewellery over the next twelve months.

II

Vincent Shaw, the highly respected agent, took up the challenge in 1974 and it began brightly enough. A guest appearance at Caesar's Palace in Luton on March 10th was a tremendous success, with the club having to close its doors on most nights. Shaw placed a half page advertisement in the trade newspaper, The Stage, advertising Kathy's services, and quoted George Savva as saying she was "A truly great star", Savva owned Caesar's Palace.

A rare West End appearance followed when she closed the first half of a star studded Variety Artistes and Children's Guild Show, presented by the Victoria Palace. The reviewer from The

Stage wrote, 'looking just the same as ever, her version of 'My Way' was the emotive moment in the evening's entertainment'.

Granada Television offered her the chance to make a comeback on the small screen, with a guest appearance alongside Frank Ifield on 'The Wheeltappers and Shunters Club', to be screened at peak viewing slot of 9.30pm on Saturday May 11th. Looking radiant that night she sang the old New Seekers hit 'You Won't Find Another Fool Like Me' and 'So Here I Go Again'. Originally released in 1971, it somehow seemed appropriate. As the reviewer for the Television Today noted 'and the best of all we had Kathy

Kirby back again. Looking blonder and more alluring than ever and with the same sideways grin. Was the voice a little huskier than it used to be? Well, none the worse for that, it added a new dimension to the warmth and to the feeling. What a pleasure it was to see her working her numbers so very professionally.

Several years later, finding myself on a television commercial with the resident host of 'Wheeltappers', the comic Bernard Manning (who I found to be a perfect gentleman, unlike his public image), I asked him what it had been like working with Kathy on that edition of the show. Bluntly he told me of all the problems she had caused on the set that day, and that he hoped he would never have to work with her again. I couldn't believe it, but of course I had yet to experience it at first hand. I caught her act again at Caesar's Palace,

Dudley on June 2nd, happy that Vincent Shaw was finding the singer better dates than she had been playing. It was all about to come to an end though. Soon after, the newspapers reported that she had lost the services of Shaw. Kathy was quoted as saying, "it was a mutual decision", and Mr Shaw would not be drawn, only stating, "Miss Kirby is an outstanding star". Reporting the break, one newspaper noted that Kathy was becoming more and more reclusive. Playing her records late into the night, alone, she would dance in front of a wall-to-wall mirror in her drawing room. Feeling lonely she would telephone friends and advisors late into the night, and naturally it would be Vincent Shaw who was disturbed from his sleep. Something I was to experience all too often in the future.

JH

III

Rumours were now circulating concerning the condition of the Kirby bank balance, which left Kathy incensed. While appearing at the Apollo restaurant in Portsmouth, she again made news by stopping her cabaret act and enquiring if there were any engaged couples in the audience that night. She thrust a £2,000 ring into the girl's hand, who was sitting near the stage. Having read of the reports that she was selling her jewellery to keep the wolf from the door, she had recently put up another ring for sale at Christie's, valued at £12,000. This was her way of hitting back at the gossips who had suggested she was a fallen star. "I've got lots of bookings" she told the Press.

However, as Lynda Lee Potter observed in the Daily Mail, 'at 33 it's time pretty Kathy dropped her image of the trusting, trembling sixteen year old with stars in her eyes, who really can't manage to cope on her own. Time that she stopped doing daft things like giving away a perfectly good £2,000 ring to a stranger just to prove she wasn't broke.' Kathy rang the journalist to let her know she agreed with her.

The strangest story which appeared in the Press around that time, was one concerning Paul Webb. A newspaper carrying a photograph of the two of them quoted Kathy as saying that they planned to marry in the November. At that point she had known him for just one week. Twenty-four hours later the tabloids carried the news that Mr Webb called to see Kathy to take her to a cabaret date in Darlington, another woman was by his side, who just happened to be his wife. He also was the father of three young children. Mr Webb, Kathy then discovered, was in fact Paul Trevillion, a freelance artist. Anyway regardless of the name change, he told the Press he was the singer's new agent and that he aimed to take her to the top again.

The story continued the following day. Kathy apparently became hysterical in the car to Darlington, following the revelations.

According to the newspapers a confrontation occurred between Kathy and Eunice, Trevillion's wife, in the singer's hotel room in Darlington. Trevillion told the Press he did not know how to handle the situation when Kathy had started talking of marriage the week before, so he just played along with it, "that's why I gave my name as Webb," he went on, "I didn't want anyone to know who I really was". But more of the saga was to follow. Kathy's 'true love', Greek Cypriot, George Stylianou, 44, drove through the night from Portsmouth to comfort Kathy. It was at his restaurant where she had given away the valuable ring. Kathy was quoted as saying, "thank goodness George came. I have never wept so much in my life. I love George and would like us to marry as soon as possible." Stylianou, with three children by his first marriage stayed silent, refusing to discuss the relationship with his second wife.

With stories like these appearing frequently now, could Kathy Kirby be taken seriously?

More front pages were full of Kathy's name, only a few days later. The £12,000 ring put up for auction at Christie's had been stolen minutes before the sale was due to take place. Taken from its case, it had been replaced by a paste imitation. Bought for her as an investment by Ambrose some ten years before, she originally had been so proud of it, that an oil painting of her in evening gown and wearing the ring, had been commissioned. It was the first time in fifteen years that anything like this had happened at

Christie's. That night, following the theft, Kathy was comforted by both Mr Webb and Mr Stylianou.

(In April of the following year, Kathy would issue a writ against the world famous auction house. Paid £6,000 on account, she was seeking the balance of £4,000, from the reserve price of £10,000).

On the following Sunday, the front pages, tongue in cheek, carried the story conclusion to the 'rings' saga. Driving back down south from a cabaret date, Kathy had with her two rings, one gold and the other a replica of the one stolen from Christie's, wrapped in a paper handkerchief. George Stylianou mistook them for rubbish and threw them out of the car window on the A1 near Portsmouth. The rings were not insured and the newspapers reported that 'Kathy was very cross!'.

IV

The last time I would see Kathy work for some considerable time, would be at the Pier Theatre, Skegness, at the beginning of September 1974. She was topping the bill in the final show of the series of 'Sunday Star Concerts', which featured a host of name acts through the season. Supporting Kathy on her bill were the comic Jimmy Marshall and guitarist Bert Weedon. On holiday with my family at that time in Bournemouth, I caught the train home on the Saturday night and drove up to Skegness with a friend the following day. I then returned to Bournemouth by train on the Monday. Such was my dedication in those days. Business was fair and I recall that night she added two new songs to her repertoire; from Jesus Christ Superstar, 'I Don't Know How To Love Him', which I never saw her include in her cabaret work again, and the recent Perry Como hit, 'It's Impossible'.

JH

1975 opened with a mixture of highs and lows for Kathy. The rumours of her financial problems turned out to be true and with mounting debts the bailiffs arrived at the Kirby household. From the post-Ambrose chaos she was left with just a bed and the carpet underlay.

The previous autumn she had been filmed by the BBC as one of three subjects, the other two being comedian and the highly respected actor, Bill Maynard, and the film star Anthony Steel. The programme was the 'Man Alive' documentary special called 'Fallen Idols'. The programme featured the three artistes talking of their days now, and the problems they encountered now that they were no longer at the top of the show business ladder. Kathy, now struggling through one night stands at small cabaret rooms (part of her segment was filmed at The Crystal Rooms, Hereford), spoke of the difficulties she had had since Ambrose died. The programme would not be broadcast until the following April, and in that January when the bailiffs arrived at the flat, and for reasons best known to Kathy, she rang the 'Man Alive' offices asking if they wanted to film her flat being stripped, as part of her story.

V

On the 29th January 1975 Kathy Kirby married for the first time. A brief romance with a former London policeman turned writer, Frederick Pye. They had known each other for three months and Fred popped the question just forty-eight hours earlier. Kathy telephoned the emergency duty registrar at Finsbury Town Hall the previous Sunday and asked if they could get married that day. The answer was no, but speedy arrangements were made and the couple were married just two days later. Kathy, wearing a cream two-piece suit, was presented with a huge bouquet of flowers just before the service, and said afterwards, "it was the most nervous moment of my life. I was petrified. It was worse than my opening night as a singer". Fred, accompanied by his two children, Kate 18 and Sarah 10, by a previous marriage, told the Press he had first met Kathy when he planned to write a book about her. The couple didn't plan a honeymoon, but they did return to Kathy's mother's home for a reception afterwards. Kathy's brother Douglas was also there to see his eldest sister married.

The wedding made the front pages of the national newspapers, together with the news of Kathy's West End cabaret comeback the following month. This would turn out to be a short season at the Celebrity Club. 'The Stage' would give Kathy her comeback review, 'it was obvious that Kathy Kirby still has a great deal to offer the business and that there is an enormous amount of affection for this talented artiste. It was unfortunate that inauspicious circumstances, including an appallingly ill mannered member of the public, and a faulty sound system, did their best to mar the show; but she battled on with courage and charm, showing that she has few peers when it comes to belting out numbers of high emotional content.'

The newly married couple settled in Brighton for a time, and trade newspapers featured advertisements offering Kathy's services, with a local telephone number and Fred's name. Living in a converted windmill on the Sussex Downs, the offers didn't exactly come pouring in, in fact the work was almost non-existent. Soon after the wedding a woman's magazine did a feature on Kathy under the headline 'Kathy Kirby, the Superstar who's been booed'. In discussion, 'she is the singer who makes everyone think twice about success, for at the age of 36 she's taken more abuse from her public than any normal person could stand'. Kathy was curiously revealing in this article. Asked if she considered herself a 'has been' she remarked, "anyone who says anything like that simply doesn't have the intelligence. I suppose it did all happen to me too young, but I've kept my magic. If you lose that, it shows in your face, and your public won't love you anymore". Asked what would happen if her career failed to take off again, she retaliated, "but it will, I know I can be better than ever, life on stage is far easier for me than it ever has been off. Always has been."

The 'Man Alive' programme aired in the May. Kathy's segment gathered most of the publicity and reviews, with many critics expressing sorrow in how her career had gone so haywire since the death of Ambrose. In the documentary Kathy spoke of how she had to grow up since her mentor's death, of how she had been manipulated, and the problems she had experienced being on her own for the first time. Horrified at the thought of seeming to want sympathy, she simply thought it was time the world knew the truth about what she had gone through since her manager had died.

Don Phillips, her long time musical director, spoke glowingly of the Kirby magic and ability. Adding that she could get all the work she wanted, she simply must prove to the business that she was reliable. Acknowledging that Kathy had a natural flair for judging an audience's mood, what she needed most was the right person to handle her. "If we could find another Bert Ambrose, she would be there," he added.

Bill Cotton, the Head of Light Entertainment for the BBC,

expressed genuine sadness at Kathy now having to scratch around for work. Sorry that Kathy had left the BBC in 1966, he said, "if someone decided to record her again and she got three hit records, she would be there. She's been there before and she won't make the same mistakes again." The BBC boss concluded, "unfortunately when people leave the BBC, it's like a divorce, they just get forgotten."

Although sympathetic in its handling of Kathy's current position, it was a television programme she would well have been advised not to appear in. From then on she was always referred to in the Press as a 'Fallen Star' or 'The Star Who Faded Away'.

Kathy in a pose so evocative of the sixties

Kathy relaxing on the set of her BBC TV series

Kathy relaxing between performances.

The author's favourite photograph of Kathy.

A highly successful three week UK tour with Tom Jones

Kathy tops the bill

More curtain calls for the golden girl, and a boat trip with Frank!

A classic theatre bill

Kathy at the height of her fame.

Kathy with her nieces at the zoo.
Claudia, now Lady Rothermere, on the right, and Sarah

Kathy on stage at the South Pier, Blackpool, towards the end of her public appearances, in 1981. A standing ovation followed.

Some nifty footwork on the Kathy Kirby Show with The Peter Gordeno dancers

Taking a break from rehearsals for The Royal Variety Performance with Cilla Black and Millicent Martin

July 1956 with Ambrose

1959, and a redhead!

Blossoming

Early days

NME Poll Winners' Concert 1964   I remember you

A rare picture of Kathy with Bert Ambrose

Where stardom began. Kathy with (left to right), Ray Martine, Vince Hill and Tommy Bruce on the set of the TV show Stars and Garters

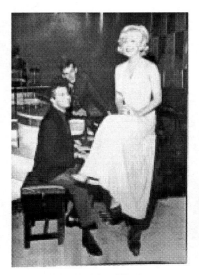

Singing with Billy Fury accompanied by Peter Nero at the piano

Kathy flying out for the 1965 Eurovision Contest being held in Naples

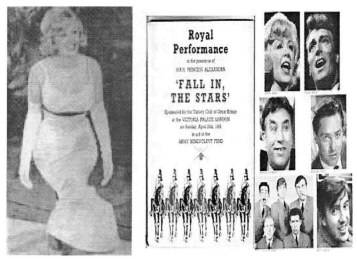

The queen of pop acknowledges the Queen of her country at the 1964 Royal Variety performance, and a programme from another Royal show in the same year, before Princess Alexandra.

Kathy and Ambrose dine out in Monte Carlo.

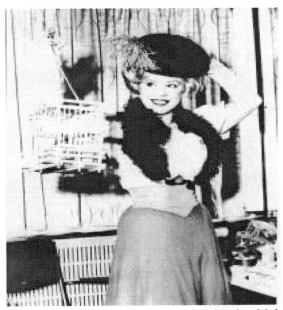

Kathy's portrayal of music hall star, Marie Lloyd, which was part of a star-studded television show to celebrate the 90th birthday of Sir Winston Churchill

Blackpool 1967, and Kathy stole the show

Kathy in 1965   The famous lip gloss

Two furry friends! Kathy and Geeki

'As years go rolling by...'

1971

1972

1974

1978

The silent star

Chapter Nine

Buddy Can You Spare A Dime

"...this lady is quite incapable of any straightforward answers."

James Tye (Official Receiver)

I

Seven months into the marriage the Press reported on how things were going. At a beauty farm called Henlow Grange in Bedfordshire, the current clientele were discussing the sudden 1.00am departure of Kathy and her husband. Hours before, the two of them could be heard 'discussing' things rather loudly, accompanied by various objects being thrown through the couple's window. A member of staff, on investigating the noise, found a mirror and a couple of windows smashed, and Fred, with blood on his face. Although they had booked for a further week's stay, they left soon afterwards. This all seemed at odds with the quote Kathy had given just days earlier, "I know people won't believe me when I say I have changed. But time will prove that at last I'm happy, sensible and secure."

An angry Fred contacted the Press the following day to put his version of events. "I walked head first into a wooden beam. The impact made me stumble and I slithered across a dressing room table and broke a window." The health farm refused to comment.

On one occasion Kathy and Fred had a heated argument while Fred was driving across London. Upset and in tears, Kathy alighted from the car at the next traffic lights. While Fred drove around in search of a parking space in order to go after his wife, a member of the public who had witnessed the heated exchange approached Kathy offering a shoulder to cry on.

Recognising Kathy immediately he asked if the guy in the car was upsetting her because if so 'he could be sorted'.

By this time Fred had parked his car and found his wife, and with a polite exchange they walked on from the stranger.

"Do you know who you were talking to?" Fred asked the singer. Kathy obviously had no idea.

Fred told her that it was an East End guy called Charlie, the older brother of the notorious twins, Reg and Ronnie Kray.

Now not working, Kathy became a full time housewife for the next eighteen months. It was soon revealed she had lost the baby she had longed for.

She said "I want a child more than anything else in the world, and the whole experience was heart breaking. I haven't recovered yet."

For many years she had believed she was unable to have children. Having undergone tests in hospital, soon afterwards she became pregnant. However, not taking enough care, while playing with her Yorkshire terrier she fell and brought on the miscarriage.

Small consolation was the thought of moving back to Mayfair in the October of that year. The champagne district where she had lived as a girl with Ambrose in 1962.

A new single was released in 1976, a disco version of the standard, 'My Prayer', and it showed her still to be in fine voice, showing her exceptional vocal range. It was released on the President label. But the best news was the announcement that she had been invited back to sing on the BBC on New Year's Eve.

At 10.30pm the corporation presented 'A Jubilee Of Music', a seventy-five minute gala programme to launch the Queen's Silver Jubilee year. On the bill were many of the artistes who, over the past twenty-five years, had contributed to popular music. Introduced by Dame Vera Lynn, these included Cliff Richard, Max Bygraves, Ken Dodd, Val Doonican and Petula Clark. Kathy looked like a million dollars that night, and her segment was shot on location, filmed on London Bridge. Introducing the film of Kathy to the studio audience, Dame Vera said, "by just mentioning the song 'Secret Love', I'm sure you will all have guessed that the next singer is Kathy Kirby'. It would prove to be her last major BBC television appearance. Her dazzling performance also hid the fact that she and Frederick Pye had just separated.

The BBC Jubilee show didn't turn out to be the start of good things to come. Indeed the early part of the year would bring further headlines concerning the singer's financial problems, and much heartache for Kathy.

The proposed move to Mayfair never took place, and the tabloids reported Kathy frantically making telephone calls everywhere, trying to trace her husband. Friends were quoted as saying 'that it was all over, and had been for some time'. Only weeks before Kathy had given an interview to one of the daily newspapers about her views on love and sex. "The man who turns me on must be in love with me, and me with him," she said in the feature, "otherwise there's no point in marriage, is there?" She made no mention of Frederick Pye.

'Singer Kathy Is In Debt To The Tune Of £24,000' was the headline that began 1977 for her. A creditors meeting in London was told that the singer owed about £24,000 and had assets of around £2,000. A resolution was passed to apply to have her judged as bankrupt, under her married name of Mrs Frederick Pye. Covering her face with a headscarf, she sat alone in a room, as it took her creditors just ten minutes to decide that her assets should be frozen, until the outcome of the hearing. The bankruptcy petition was presented by two officials from the Inland Revenue, to whom Kathy owed £16,187. The Official Receiver, James Tye, later said that the balance was alleged to be owed to other creditors. One of these was her former manager, Bill Preston, who had by this time successfully sued her for full back wages from the 1971 Blackpool season. Kathy, following the meeting, gave a short Press statement announcing that she hoped to sort things out during the next six months and with some money to come she didn't think it would go to court. How wrong she was.

Now living in a rented flat in the Barbican, the papers all carried Kathy's next court appearance. On June 22nd she duly told the court of her 'missing millions'. "I had a home worth half a million, investments, diamonds, minks and property. But they have all gone now," she said. Kathy promised to pay her debts of almost £18,000, mostly to the taxman, and added that she believed that a good deal of her fortune had been embezzled. "It's amazing how ruthless some people can be when a girl is on her own," she would tell the Press. Given a five-month reprieve, the receiver told her "you do the singing and I'll work with the tax people." She still had forthcoming dates in Aldershot, Leeds and Newcastle, and at this point in her career could still command £1,200 per week in cabaret. Kathy left court knowing that the debt was mostly against tax assessments, something, which she never appealed.

Now living on a controlled budget fixed by her mother (Eileen was in court with her), Kathy also told the Press of her crumbling marriage, and that she had begun divorce proceedings.

III

Four months later in November, just before Kathy was due back in court to give a progress report on her efforts to pay her debts, the headlines screamed, 'Kathy Kirby's Hard-Up Husband Is Missing'. Fred Pye had vanished with debts totally more than £10,000. At the same court at which Kathy appeared it was indicated that the receiver would have to apply for a warrant to have Pye arrested. All attempts to find him had failed.

A receiving order was made against him at Kathy's flat in the Barbican. However, the singer told the officials that she believed her missing husband was now living in Islington. That address, however, turned out to be the home of his parents, and Kathy had secretly told friends she thought Fred might now be in Italy where he had property.

Before her own appearance in court, she was involved in yet another domestic incident, which gave her more unfavourable Press.

Actor and dancer, Denny Ryder, and his wife Roma, spoke of popping over to see Kathy with a bottle of wine and 'lots of sympathy', hearing about her recent problems. Ryder, having known Kathy for more than ten years spent the evening pleasantly reminiscing. According to the actor, when it reached 2.00am in the morning they felt it best to leave. What followed, claimed Ryder, was 'thirty minutes of hell'. Suddenly Kathy lost her composure and attacked the two of them, giving Ryder a black eye. Escaping from the flat, he asked the hall porter to call the police. Spending thirty minutes at Wood Street police station being questioned, the singer was eventually released and a police spokesman said their inquiries were continuing. Naturally Kathy's version in the newspaper the following day was rather different. She told of how the couple had sat drinking over two bottles of wine, while listening to her records. Kathy's story was that Roma accused her husband of flirting with her and they started bickering. Kathy, on asking them to leave, found they refused, so she tried to call the police. She went on to say that Ryder ripped the telephone from her hand, hit her over the head with it and twisted her arm, then Roma grabbed her hair. Whatever version is true, it was certainly some black eye that Denny sported for the national Press the next day.

Kathy appeared in court the day after the latest 'domestic incident' to give her progress report.

At the latest appearance, Friday November 11th, Kathy had blamed six men for her financial downfall. Ambrose topped the list with the singer stating, "Bert was to blame for discrepancies in my bank balance. I tried not to bring a revered personal memory into it, but I find my reputation worsening." She went on to point the finger at her estranged husband who she, "had stupidly let look after her tax affairs"; her brother-in-law Terry, who had acted

111

as her financial advisor, (Kathy claimed that he had issued cheques on her bank account without her knowledge); and an unnamed accountant who she claimed had told her in 1970 that all her money had gone, when only two years earlier she was worth over a million pounds. Revealing that the accountant had upset her by making her earnings appear lower than they really had been, she was warned by the receiver that should that be true, she might owe even more tax. The two other men to let her down, she claimed, were a bank manager and a solicitor. "I have been harassed, embezzled and swindled", she told the court. Warned several times about the way she replied to questions, Kathy left the court hiding tears, consoled at least for the time that she had avoided the bankruptcy stigma.

Kathy had been told to hand over the contents of a private safe, which had not been opened since the death of Ambrose in 1971, for only he knew the combination. Previously, she had obstructed the receiver's agents when they had tried to enter her flat, for which she was now reprimanded. She was given fourteen days to give them access and should she fail to do so an order to seize her assets would be made. Her next appearance was adjourned until January 13th 1978, giving her twenty-eight days to produce an account of her spending.

It was at this appearance that she made a strange offer to the court. At the hearing, the singer mentioned a mysterious letter that had been submitted to the court, which Kathy explained, was a financial offer to cover her debts. Registrar Barbury replied, "I wish you hadn't mentioned that letter. It was a gross impertinence. It is now in the waste paper basket. I have tried to shut it out of my mind."

The amount offered was not made public, but Mr Barbury did remark, "I wonder myself if you know what you are talking about", adjourning the case again until April 19th. Outside the court Kathy tried to show the Press the contents of the letter. It was on headed notepaper from the Kendall Medical Incorporation of Santa Monica, California. Explaining that it contained an offer to the court from her business manager, a Doctor Kendall, Kathy had the letter snatched from her hands by a Denis Kendall, who denied being her business manager. As he walked off he told her she "was a first class idiot". Asked by the Press why the letter had been sent to the court, Kathy explained that she really didn't know, other than trying to show she was doing something to clear her debts.

On the eve of the next court date, on the 19th, Mr James Tye and his staff went to Kathy's flat with a seizure order. Although a police officer was present, Kathy refused to let them in. Smashing a window to gain entry, the singer became hysterical and threw a hairbrush at them. A woman officer was summoned to sit with the sobbing star in her bedroom whilst the flat was searched. Mr

Tye discovered many items, which Kathy had not disclosed to the court. His staff was ordered to take away carpets, chandeliers, and jewellery, furniture, furnishings, a mink coat and a safe. Kathy was left with her stereo, records and sheet music. She was devastated.

Too ill to actually attend the court the next day, her counsel produced a doctor's note and pleaded for one last chance for the star to explain her financial situation. The court, understandably refused, and Kathy was branded a liar, (something the Press seized on for their headlines) stating that she had not been truthful on several occasions about her assets. The Registrar, satisfied that Kathy had failed to make a full and truthful disclosure, adjourned the public examination 'sine die', which meant she would be unable to apply for discharge from bankruptcy until her examination was restored.

It took the cracksman, on the authority of the court, two hours to break open the safe. Kathy, who had hoped it would be full of money, was told of the outcome. It was completely empty. Disappointed though she was, she was more occupied at the time at being branded a liar. She told the press. "that is the one thing I am not. I have never been called a liar and I will not be called one now."

IV

The first lady of Fleet Street, Jean Rook, wrote a double-page interview with Kathy days after the last court appearance, with a photograph of the singer showing the glamour of 1971, as she appeared then. Now the face was one of despair, a stone and a half under weight. She answered all the difficult questions Miss Rook put to her, giving her the now well known theories of everyone, from Ambrose to Frederick Pye embezzling her money, and of how she had been too trusting. Miss Rook wondered how someone approaching middle age could be so simple. Asking the journalist at the end of the interview if she ever showed the people she quizzed a copy of the finished article. Kathy answered the question herself, "no, I suppose not, so what's the point of worrying". The conclusion to the article read, "but you won't make me sound icky, or as if I'm always asking for money will you?", asked Miss Kirby, (who didn't ask the Express for a penny). "I can trust you, can't I?", she said at the door of her flat. "You can Miss Kirby, but will you ever learn that you shouldn't?"

Following the piece, the newspaper published many letters from Kirby fans wishing her well.

In June, Kathy's £2,600 a year flat in the Barbican was repossessed by the City of London Corporation. The following month, July 27th, she was rushed to the Middlesex Hospital, and later transferred to St. Luke's, with another drug overdose. Now homeless and out of work, Kathy was under heavy sedation, with her mother at her bedside.

She would later deny she tried to kill herself, blaming a £15 lobster she had prepared. She said it had made her ill and she had fainted soon after eating it.

Meanwhile, yet another agent thought it was time she was given another chance. Reuben Freeman and Ronnie Ball of International Theatre Promotions secured a couple of television spots in Holland, and cabaret dates at such places as Torquay's Doddles Club, The Roundabout Club, Newport and the Sheppey Villa Club. As ever, the new business relationship wasn't to survive the summer.

Kathy moved back to her mother's home in Essex, following the departure from her flat and the hospital stay. With no work in her diary a rift soon developed between the two of them. Her divorce came through in January 1979 and very shortly afterwards Kathy left the family home. After one argument too many, the singer stormed out of the house and booked herself into a hotel in London. The impulsive move would lead to one of the blackest moments in her life, and the Press headlines far outstripped what had gone before.

Chapter Ten

Once I Had A Secret Love

"My daughter is a very sick girl, she needs help.

Eileen Kirby

I

Kathy Kirby booked herself into the Mount Royal Hotel in London to discuss a fresh start with a businessman, whom she thought wanted to invest some £150,000 in her career. Booked into the hotel by the man, Ian Bestwick, and his wife, they paid for the first two nights. Bestwick and his wife departed after discussing various options with Kathy, and the singer proceeded to stay on for a further nine days. Unable to pay, Kathy was charged with deception and obtaining credit while an undischarged bankrupt. The hotel contacted Eileen, regarding the rest of her daughter's bill, but she refused to pay. As she told the Press, "I've done everything to help her, and I love her, but she keeps telling me that I'm not her mother anymore. She's terribly upset and confused and I'm trying to get her medical treatment."

With Eileen refusing to pay the bill, the police were called. Kathy was arrested by two policemen at the hotel. She asked them if they could leave by a backdoor as she didn't wish anyone to see her go. The police, however, told her that there were only tourists in the foyer area at present, so it wasn't likely she would be recognised. The three of them left for the station through the main foyer.

Kathy spent the evening in a police cell. The following morning she pleaded not guilty at London's Marlborough Street magistrate's court, to a charge of deception, and obtaining accommodation worth £308.83. She was remanded on bail until the case could be heard on May 21st. It was the condition of the bail, however, that would make the headlines the following day. As the court was told she was homeless, she was ordered to stay at St. Luke's Mental Hospital in Muswell Hill. The magistrate, Mr St John Harmsworth, having been told Kathy had nowhere to go, said at least it would provide a roof over her head. Charged under her real name of Katherine Pye, her counsel, Mr Stephen Ruttel, told the court she would be prepared to spend two weeks at the hospital until alternative accommodation could be found. Mr Harmsworth retorted; "your client is in no position to bargain. She is at the mercy of the court."

Seeing the news coverage, I was close to tears. Letters from the singer's fans and admirers flooded into the pages of the newspapers. Offers of accommodation, holidays, small amounts of money, and general support all came from the public. I was horrified. There wasn't much I could do, however,

I did get a friend to drive me down to London where I purchased a large bouquet of flowers and personally delivered them to the mental home, with a note wishing her well.

JH

Fred Pye was quoted from his new home in Italy. Although he told the Press she had cost him a great deal of money, he seemed genuinely saddened that she had ended up where she was. He didn't believe, however, that his ex-wife now had the will to make a new career. Having lived the life of the Hollywood stars that she had seen in films, she was totally incapable of handling life when it went wrong. He concluded, "I'd love to see her bounce back, but it won't happen."

Kathy had been placed in a ward with acutely disturbed people. The singer had been given little choice by the court but to make the best of it. Allowed out for just a few hours each day, Kathy had few visitors, and spent her time reading the never-ending letters, best wishes and get well cards that arrived for her daily.

Kathy stayed at the hospital until the beginning of April, when she appeared in court, asking that the conditions of her bail be dropped. On the 4th Mr Harmsworth released her from the hospital, admitting there had been a mix-up. "I think it was suggested as a suitable place," he told Kathy, "I then found out sometime later it was a mental hospital". Hearing she had been placed in a ward with patients who had severe psychiatric problems, he agreed with Kathy's counsel that she could stay with a woman friend, with unconditional bail until her next court date at Wells Street on May 21st.

Kathy allowed herself a smile as the magistrate told the singer, "I am glad to see you are better. You have afforded the people of this country a great deal of pleasure in the past."

On May 21st Kathy elected to go to trail by jury, and was committed to Knightsbridge Magistrates Court for a date to be announced. She was granted legal aid.

II

The woman friend Kathy was allowed to stay with would be the cause of the most scandalous headlines the singer had ever faced. The news broke in the December of that year.

Her name was Laraine McKay, and she was a great fan of the star. Upset that Kathy had been forced to stay in the mental home, Miss McKay sent the singer a bouquet of flowers with a note attached. The next day she visited her favourite singer. She was in her late twenties, dark-hair, cut short, with blue eyes. She also seemed to dress like a boy, wearing trousers and a man's anorak. On that first visit she stayed an hour and returned the following day with two hundred carnations.

Her visits to the hospital became frequent after that, and Kathy, with little contact with the outside world, would look forward to seeing Laraine. During the four months she remained in hospital, the two women drew closer, and if for any reason Laraine could not visit, she would send Kathy letters. The fan also left her a bag of coins in order that she would be able to telephone her.

When Kathy brought up the subject that the only way she was going to be allowed to leave was if she was offered somewhere to live, Laraine jumped at the chance of helping. A room in her own family home could be provided. With the magistrate's permission, Kathy went to live in Laraine's home in New Barnet, with her married sister and children.

Initially Kathy had her own bedroom, and she was quite happy there. However, soon after the two women took a long weekend holiday in Brighton, the relationship became sexual. Kathy, confused, resisted at first, but how could she reject her now? The only person who had shown her kindness, had listened to her problems and offered her a way out of the mental home. She had to reciprocate. In any case she felt safe with her. It was not fulfilling, but gradually regular lovemaking became part of their lives.

Eileen objected strongly, and tried to break up the relationship, but Kathy was losing touch with reality by now. Although she wanted to return to the stage, there were no bookings and she was surviving on £16 a week from unemployment benefits.

Kathy now claims that Laraine had virtually absorbed her mind, and emotionally she had lost the will to think for herself. That December the fan asked her favourite singer to marry her, Kathy, totally stunned, didn't know what to say at first, she wasn't even sure two people of the same sex could marry. Laraine explained that several of her gay friends had gone through a service of 'bonding'.

Not wanting to upset her, Kathy agreed. Unfortunately in her excitement Laraine told a number of her friends. One of these telephoned the newspapers in the hope of making a few pounds out of the story. Every newspaper carried the event as its lead story the following day, 'Kathy Kirby To Marry Woman'. The date they planned was December 5th. Stating that the two of them had their wedding cleared by the Chelsea Registry Office, Kathy went on. "this is true love. I know it. I'm not concerned about what any of my fans, or anyone else might think about our relationship. Laraine was one of the few people who came to visit me while I was in the hospital earlier this year, and our relationship just flowered from then on."

Baffled officials at the Registry Office claimed to know nothing of the proposed ceremony, and it was pointed out, Kathy hadn't even been to see them to discuss the matter. Besides, they added, it wasn't possible to marry two women, it was not legal in this country. The official concluded his statement to the press, warning that the singer could find herself open to possible prosecution for perjury.

The later editions of the newspapers told the sorry conclusion to the story. Hours after posing for celebratory photographs with Kathy, Laraine was arrested on two charges involving cheques, to the value of £8,000 and £10,000. She was now languishing in Holloway Prison. It transpired that she had first been in court on these charges the previous September and had been released on bail. Laraine's mother and brother refused to continue to stand bail as a protest to the wedding plans, so with her sureties withdrawn, she had been arrested.

Eileen Kirby spoke of her grief of what was happening to her daughter. Of the shock of being told of the lesbian relationship, and the horror of being told, "Mummy, I'm going to marry Laraine."

An openly weeping Kathy told the Press. "I would be getting married now, if only the police would let Laraine out of jail. I'm so unhappy. Laraine is my Prince Charming and I'm very worried about her." Speaking of how much she could see of Ambrose in the girl, she said, "I truly love her, as much as I ever loved Bert."

Kathy moved out of Laraine's family home and booked into the hotel where the two of them should have celebrated their wedding. The champagne reception organised by Laraine remained untouched, Kathy was alone in her suite.

III

On the February 6th 1981, Laraine McKay, who gave her occupation as a florist, appeared in court admitting twenty charges of fraud and forgery, involving almost £30,000. Sentenced to three years, she later told a bankruptcy hearing that she spent a good deal of money on hotel bills, clothes and jewellery for her singer. The money had come from swindling gullible businessmen. Admitting to debts of £27,500, she told the receiver, Mr John O'Reilly, that some £5,000 had been lost on gambling, but the vast amount, and her bankruptcy, resulted almost entirely from her gifts to Kathy. The court heard she was in love and totally infatuated with the singer. Following the court appearance Laraine was returned to prison to complete her sentence.

Chapter Eleven

Maybe This Time

"Why would I be talking to you like this if I wanted to walk away from my career?"

Kathy Kirby

I

1980 began with Kathy trying to kick-start her career once more. With the help of Ian Bestwick, she made her first appearance in over a year, singing in a bingo hall in Chatham, Kent. Performing a thirty-minute spot between sessions of the game. She was rewarded by a standing ovation and shouts of 'more' by the six hundred bingo players who had paid 30p to see the act. Said Kathy, "It may not be much of a start, but I had to begin somewhere, and it could not have gone much better than this. I was overjoyed at the way the audience treated me. I must admit, I cried, they were really wonderful." With Ian Bestwick at her side she began to pick up the pieces and made cabaret appearances, at such places as The Tudor House in Bearstead in Kent.

The working relationship didn't survive long into the year and Mr Bestwick departed. With no work on the book, the only bright spot was in October when she was finally cleared of cheating the

Mount Royal Hotel out of £304. Now, living again with her mother, Kathy appeared at Knightsbridge Crown Court pleading not guilty to charges of deception. After legal submission, Judge John Bolland directed the jury to acquit her, stating that, because she had been booked into the hotel by friends, she was not liable for the bill. He concluded that Kathy, other than staying in the hotel and using their services, had done nothing to obtain credit, indeed, the hotel had given her credit. Ian Bestwick told the court, 'I felt she was a very fine artiste and her career, at that particular time, was being wasted. It was my hope that Kathy would renew her career and I would give her as much help as possible." It was not to be.

II

One week later Kathy sold her story to a leading Sunday newspaper.

She told of the time, a few years back, when destitute, she was forced to leave her Barbican flat and spend the night homeless, huddled in a shop doorway. Of how, with her last few coins, she rang her former colleagues for help. Lord Delfont was 'on the other line', neither Billy Marsh, the agent, or Eric Morley could help. And her former publicity agent didn't want to know. In the end she did what she vowed she would never do again; Kathy went home to her mother. She spoke of her four-month ordeal in the mental home, when the patients were often sedated to protect not only themselves, but also each other. Of feeling totally forgotten until a letter came for her one day, from Paul and Linda McCartney, with £500 in twenty pound notes. Paul had written a note hoping the money would help in some way. Years before he had written a song for Kathy, called 'Honey Pie'. She never recorded it though, as Kathy's advisors at the time didn't feel it was right for her.

She spoke of the regret of staying with Ambrose, of having to choose between him and Bruce Forsyth. It was obvious she felt very strongly for the entertainer at the time, and still held him very affectionately in her memory.

She revealed for the first time, at the height of her fame, she became pregnant by Ambrose, forty years her senior. Not telling either him, or her mother, she had an abortion. She knew Ambrose would refuse to marry her, as he had often said it wouldn't look good to her fans. It didn't stop him taking her money, though, to feed his gambling habit. Towards the end of his life Kathy would also discover he was stealing her jewellery, to pawn it, and pay off his bad debts. When he died in 1971 her manager had stolen and gambled away most of her estimated five million pound earnings.

The icing on the cake was the singer's version of her relationship with Laraine McKay. Her explanation was that, by this time, she was divorced from reality, and responded to the only person who seemed to care for her. When Laraine was taken to Holloway it gave Kathy the breathing space she needed, to see in what direction she wanted to go. The tables now turned, Kathy visited Laraine in prison, giving her what comfort she could. After a couple of visits Kathy told her that they couldn't go on living together. She had to try and rebuild her career, and besides, she still realised how important men were in her life. She was not a lesbian.

As Kathy was quoted in the three-week series of features: "Men are important in my life and I'm afraid they always will be...

"It started when I was 16. That's when I lost my virginity, to someone who has since become famous in the entertainment world.

I was just starting with Bert Ambrose's band at the time and this man had been chatting up both my sister and me for a while. I don't think he could make up his mind between us,so I made it up for him.

When he hemmed me in my theatre dressing room one night I just locked the door so we wouldn't be disturbed. You only lose your virginity once!

So that was my first love and I was tugging on his shirt tails for weeks after, until Bert Ambrose intervened and cooled me down."

The article re-hashed the Tom Jones story, the rumour of their baby, and the poison pen letters she had received. Tributes were also paid to Sandie Shaw, her contemporary from the sixties, as Miss Shaw alone was the only one of Kathy's colleagues to visit her.

The three-week series ended with Kathy's hope of being given another chance to sing. That opportunity was in fact just around the corner, at the beginning of 1981.

III

The Sunday newspapers reported that Kathy had signed a new recording contract, and was to star in a feature film based on her life story. Gavin Dare, the director of Celebrity Records, who at the time had Harry Secombe and Peters and Lee on the books, told the Press, 'We are treating her like the star we believe she is. The public always had a tremendous amount of sympathy for her." Announcing that her new manager was Bruce Benson, the Press were told that 'Secret Love' was to be re-recorded in a new format, and that a new album was being set up featuring old and new songs. In the end, once more, neither was ever recorded.

President Records would release Kathy's last single in the spring of 1981. A magnificent version of Charles Aznavour song "She", which for obvious reasons became, "He". It showed Kathy in splendid voice. Very heavily played on all the major radio stations, it sold better than any other Kirby record had in years. It was just unfortunate that the B-side was the truly dreadful, "Nobody Loves Me Like You Do", which had also backed her previous President single, 'My Prayer', in 1976.

A rare television appearance was offered by Thames TV. An

interview on the afternoon magazine programme 'Afternoon Plus', with Simon Reed. Screening an old black and white clip of Kathy singing. 'I'll Get By' from an old 'Thank Your Lucky Stars' show. Newspaper clippings appeared next on screen, showing her stormy career. The camera panned onto Kathy's face, who looked as pretty as ever. Certainly it didn't show all she had gone through during the past decade. She spoke with feeling, of the bankruptcy, the broken marriage, the lesbian relationship, the embezzlement of her money and the reputation she now had of being 'difficult', and a 'prima donna'. Totally rejecting this idea, Simon Reed asked if the problem was that she expected too much perfection from everyone around her? Kathy retorted, 'Well, that says a lot about show business today then, doesn't it?' The interview ended with Kathy plugging her weekly concert dates in Skegness and Simon wished the blonde singer well for the future. It was very obvious he meant it. 'He' played over the closing credits of the show.

She next appeared on Pete Murray's 'Open House' Radio 2 programme. Before a packed house at the Capital Theatre, Horsham, she opened to a tremendous ovation with 'Secret Love', followed by 'Let Me Go Lover'. When the applause finally died down, she chatted happily of her comeback plans with the host. Telling his listeners what a rough time Kathy had had of late, the audience cheered when Pete Murray said how well she looked now, and what a pleasure it was to have her back in the spotlight.

She concluded her spot, singing her new record, 'He', which drew wild applause at the end. Pete Murray said to his audience, 'this girl makes me cry when she sings, she's tremendous'. He then turned to Kathy and told her how much the audience loved her, (which drew more applause), and that he hoped it wouldn't be too long before she was back on the television screen; something the radio audience obviously agreed with as well.

Soon after the broadcast it was announced that Pete's wife, Trisha, would be working with Kathy on her autobiography. Nothing came of it.

Another broadcast of Kathy's around this time, was David Hamilton's programme. This edition was broadcast live from the Ideal Home Exhibition. Not wanting to discuss past problems, she briefly mentioned the 'colossal void' she had felt after the death of Ambrose, and of how she cracked up. She would not be drawn to talk in depth about all her recent problems. Busy signing autographs, she spoke of the loyalty of her fans, and the warmth she had always felt from her audiences. As with Pete Murray, she mentioned her forthcoming Skegness dates, and the interview closed with the DJ playing her new release.

The weekly shows in Skegness never happened. She appeared once, on Sunday July 12th, to an enthusiastic audience. Returning for one last time on August 2nd, to close the first half of the bill, headed by Paul Shane, then at the height of his success with 'Hi De Hi'.

Naturally I attended both shows. It had been a few years since I had last seen Kathy work, and I was rather worried what to expect. Seeing the shows I could not believe how well she looked, and how great she sounded. Maybe, I thought, something wonderful was at last around the corner.

IV

By the end of the summer, Bruce Benson had departed, and Kathy was on her own again. The London agent and impresario, Barrie Stacey, was presenting a couple of Sunday Star concerts at the South Pier, Blackpool, for the illumination crowds, during October. He was looking for a special guest star for his forthcoming 'Don Maclean Show', and I suggested Kathy to him. Barrie thought it was a great idea and contacted her immediately. She had always had a fond regard for the resort and jumped at the chance of playing the town again.

The talented Birmingham comic, Don Maclean, had always been underrated, however, I did not personally feel that he ever had a big enough name to top a bill over Kathy. His billing on the advertising leaflets was 'from BBC Television's 'Crackerjack', and that was some years past now. I went up to Blackpool for the weekend to catch the show and noticed that the local newspapers with featured articles were concentrating on Kathy's appearance. 'A Golden Girl Bounces

Back' and 'The Dance On Girl Returns', were some of the headlines. Chatting up the girls in the box office, they told me that generally the public were asking for tickets to see Kathy and not for the official star of the bill.

JH

Kathy unfortunately, had car problems, driving with Bob Barter, her new musical director, up from London. Arriving with less than an hour before curtain up, and given a police escort through Blackpool, the public were kept waiting outside the theatre while she quickly went through her band call. It was clear looking around the audience huddled in the foyer that the Kathy fans were out in force. The general conversation was of Kathy, the bad times of the past few years, and how many felt they should come along 'to support her'.

Announced, she walked on the stage to wild applause. She was a great success that night. Moved by the ovation her act received, she told the crowd that returning to Blackpool was 'just like coming home'. Her act had not really changed since the early seventies and by this time her fans knew her repertoire as well as she did. Opening with 'Without A Song', she followed with a powerful version of 'Maybe This Time'. Depending on her mood she would then sing, 'Havah Nagilah' or 'Sometimes I'm Happy'. This time she would chose the former, although Barrie Stacey had asked her to sing something else as Don Maclean would be singing it in the second half of the show. She refused. Following 'My Yiddishe Momma', she would perform a medley of her past hits and then 'Without You' would bring her false tabs. Coming back on stage she would go into 'New York, New York' an then 'He'. She would introduce her next number with the words; 'and now a song that has been done to death. If I might be so bold. 'My Way'. No one has ever milked the Paul Anka song quite the way Kathy did. That night and many others, running off stage at the end of the number, she always knew exactly how long to stay in the wings before returning to simply say, 'Yes, I did it My Way'. As always she would close her act with the song she would dedicate to her fans, 'My Thanks To You'.

I left my seat in the second row in the interval, not returning for the second half. Before going, however, I noticed a young man wildly applauding in the seat immediately in front of me. I would learn later that his name was Mark Littlemore, and he was trying to get her fan club re-launched. Not being old enough to remember Kathy during the peak period of her career, he later told me that he saw her on the BBC Jubilee programme, a couple of years back, and from that moment had been hooked.

JH

V

1982 opened with Kathy successfully applying for her discharge from bankruptcy. Skipping out of court, she found herself bumping into three policemen with a warrant for her arrest. It was issued for non-payment of rates on her former flat in the Barbican. Kathy was, however, freed, after settling the debt at the Official Receiver's Office.

Now being managed by an agency called 'Spheres', she found a lucrative market for her services in the gay clubs of London and the provinces.

It was to one of these Earls Court clubs that I travelled down to that night, with a large heart shaped box of chocolates under my arm. Well it was Valentine's Day.

JH

Also there that night was a film crew from the BBC's Nationwide, who were producing a series of films of people who had once dominated their chosen profession, and having fallen from grace, were now fighting back. When the film was shown a few weeks later, besides being given a run-down on Kathy's turbulent career, and an interview with the star in her flat, it also showed part of her cabaret performance that night at the gay club.Unfortunately, on making her entrance that night, and commencing to sing her opening number, 'Without A Song', she stopped, not at all happy with the sound systems. 'Hold it', she told the live band, 'I said hold it. Is this the BBC? Where is the soundman? I sound like Pinky and Perky". Not the best of starts perhaps, but as the Nationwide reporter remarked. 'even after an opening like that, the trouper she is, she gave them her all. And the audience in Earls Court loved her.'

Chapter Twelve

I'm Still Here

"James! Why have you never popped backstage to see me before?"

Kathy Kirby

I

The week of April 26th, I was on tour in a play, and that particular week I was appearing at the King's Theatre, Southsea. On the Friday evening Kathy was due to perform in a late night cabaret in nearby Southampton. Having played the lovely King's Theatre many times over the years, I had made some good friends in the area, and that night six of us scrambled into a car to drive over to Southampton to see Kathy in action. As always I took a bouquet of flowers and left them at the club's reception.

Arriving at the club just before cabaret time, I popped to the lavatory before the show was due to begin. I couldn't believe who I saw waiting at the top of the stairs, waiting to be announced before her spot. It was Kathy. I'd never been this close to her before. Dressed in a purple chiffon trouser suit, she looked as pretty as she had been in her heyday.

Smiling at me, I gave what I suppose was an idiotic grin and feeling my legs about to collapse under me, dashed to the loo.

She was in brilliant form that night, and with Don Phillips backing her, she felt confident enough to sing a number of stage songs she hadn't performed in years, including her sensational version of 'No Regrets'. None of my friends from Southsea had seen Kathy work before, so I was pleased they had witnessed her in such good shape. About to leave the club at the end of the night, a couple of gentlemen on reception stopped me and asked if I was James Harman. Curious, but confirming who I was, they informed me that Kathy would like to see me in her dressing room upstairs. More than a little shocked, I didn't think it was such a good idea, however, all my friends urged me on. "Well, perhaps, just for five minutes." I heard myself saying, "Will you wait for me in the bar?"

At that moment in my life I had been in the entertainment industry for eight years, and had worked with some of the biggest names in the business. To me, they were just other artistes, some nice and some others not so nice. However, as the show business journalist, Patrick Newley had observed, "almost everyone with a theatrical bent has one artiste that they love and cherish. Many times there are no reasons for this, but one star claims their devotion." I was now walking up the steps of that club to meet mine.

I can't honestly remember much of what happened that night, other than Kathy thanking me for the flowers, and asking me why I hadn't popped backstage to see her before, at any of the other concerts I had attended over the years. I remember that Don Phillips was in the room and that the five minutes I promised my friends stretched into almost an hour, while Kathy and I chatted. In the end we swapped telephone numbers and I promised to give her a call on my return to Birmingham on the Sunday. Apparently I spent the journey back from Southampton to Southsea fast asleep, with my head on the lap of my good friend, Wendy Tyrrell, a silly grin on my face.

We spoke a good deal on the telephone after that night. Sometimes Kathy would be in a good mood, other times, not so happy. She continued playing the gay clubs such as 'Seline's' and 'Elton's Discotheque' in London. She gathered a good deal of publicity when she was the star attraction at the grand opening of 'Harpoon Louis', a luxurious up-market venue in Earls Court.

By letters and telephone calls I got to know Mark Littlemore. He was busy in Manchester, trying to get Kathy's fan club started again. We arranged to meet in Chesterfield on June 6th at the Pomegranate Theatre, where Kathy was *topping a variety bill presented by Barrie Stacey. For once, bookings were not so good that night, indeed, Barrie's proposed 'Jess Conrad Show', the previous Sunday, had been cancelled, and now Jess was closing the first half of Kathy's show.*

As always the local Press were hovering around, armed with a collection of old cuttings, wanting an interview with the star. In the end the large piece was friendly enough, headlined: 'I Think I Was Surrounded By Corruption', said Kathy Kirby, 'Sweeping Back That Famous Blonde Hair'. The article didn't fail to mention that halfway through the interview a full-scale row erupted between Kathy and her mother, on just who was to blame for the singer's missing money and subsequent bankruptcy.

Her old fans were there that night, armed with old record sleeves they wanted signing. Kathy, just as in Blackpool, arrived an hour late for her rehearsal so the run through was very tight.

JH

II

The Stage newspaper would review the show the following week, under the headline. 'An Embarrassing Experience For All'.

'It would be pleasing to report that Kathy Kirby's one night stand at the Pomegranate Theatre suggested a possible change in fortune for this talented artiste. Regrettably, her unwarranted verbal lashing of the supporting musicians, and other caustic comments, proved a totally embarrassing experience for the on stage performers and audience alike. When one remembers the attractive bubbly personality of the sixties, it seems a real tragedy that such a promising career should have deteriorated in this way, for she has lost none of her power and tone in her voice, with numbers like 'Secret Love' and 'Dance On', coming over as fresh as ever. The inclusion of 'My Way' in the brief programme, and the reference to Judy Garland, seemed rather unfortunate in the circumstances.'

As a loyal fan, I wrote to the newspaper's letters page, giving what I believe to be a truer version of the night in Chesterfield.

"...the headline taken from the review referred to Kathy Kirby's unhappiness with the musicians handling of a couple of her numbers, and her mentioning it on stage. Certainly it wasn't an 'unwarranted verbal lashing' as stated by your critic, for she was firm but quite polite. Having seen Kathy on stage countless times, the backing didn't sound at all right on certain numbers, for whatever reasons. (Kathy had in fact stopped the introduction of the song 'Sometimes I'm Happy' three times, as she wasn't happy with the tempo), and certainly she didn't question the musicians' ability, as was the implication. While your reviewer was generous to mention she had lost

none of her power and tone of voice, and that her numbers
came over as fresh as ever, he could also have reported that
she got a very warm reception from the audience, with many
giving her a standing ovation at the end of her act.
Incidentally, 'her brief programme', as stated, consisted of
fifteen numbers.'

I gave Kathy a gold crucifix and chain that night, and
after the show she chatted happily to Mark and myself at the
bar, often interrupted by fans wanting her autograph.

JH

III

A rare television appearance was offered to Kathy, on the
B.A. Robertson's chat show. 'B.A. In Music' on BBC1. In an
interview which made painful viewing, the host's first question
amounted to little more than telling his guest that she was old
fashioned, even at the height of her fame. Not an experienced
television interviewer, his series had been criticised by both public
and the Press for his style. Kathy seemed an odd choice for a
show when his main interests, and guest, were contemporary
sounds. Kathy, not sure how to handle his style, and flippant way,
seemed very vulnerable. All the reviews the next day felt the
interview had been uncomfortable to watch.

A Greek restaurant in Birmingham called 'Andreas' was,

at this time, featuring the occasional 'Star' cabaret attraction. Having seen that they had just had Lonnie Donegan, I called in and asked if they would be interested in having Kathy appear in their venue. The owner was very taken with the idea, so I rang Kathy and asked what she thought. Once again, without either a manger or an agent, she left the details for me to sort out. A fee was agreed, and I set about writing the Press releases for the date, September 8th. The Birmingham newspaper seemed very interested in the return of Kathy Kirby to the Midlands, and as various subsequent articles reported, it would be the singer's first Birmingham date since playing 'La Dolce Vita' back in 1972.

Sporting a heavy cold, she refused to speak to either the Press or Central Television, who had sent a film crew. However, she was a big success that evening, playing before a capacity crowd. Following her spot at the restaurant I had arranged for her to appear the same night in midnight cabaret, at a leading gay club in the city. The Nightingale, with her voice now badly affected with a sore throat and temperature. However, she just about got through the second stint of the evening. The local Birmingham Evening Mail summed it up the following day. 'Singer Kathy Kirby, appeared at two sell out venues in the city last night. A queue of fans formed for autographs, including two men who travelled from the Isle of

Man to see her.'

A little while later another booking for her came my way. A close friend, Maurice Landis, was organising a 'Star Parade' at the South Pier, Southsea, in the November. After a unisex fashion show and disco, he was looking for a 'star' name to provide the cabaret. Naturally I suggested Kathy. My other friends in the area had told him how well she had done in nearby Southampton, the previous spring, so he seemed delighted to book her. It was a large venue to fill, with little or no holidaymakers around at that time of year. But, as the press reported, within two days of announcing Kathy's name, Maurice had sold 300 tickets. By the time of the actual show, on November 15th, it had sold out.

She was a great success again that evening, and during the next few months we would speak a lot on the telephone. I suddenly had this crazy idea one night, once my pantomime season was over, I might just be the one to successfully manage her. It seems silly now, looking back, that I could have thought of it, let alone considered it seriously. How could I, with no management experience, have succeeded when all the other agents and managements of the last decade had failed.

Anyway, in the New Year, I called to see her at her London flat and mentioned it to her. Kathy seemed all for the idea, really pleased, so I set about getting organised.

New photographs were reproduced, a new biography made up and mass-produced, and I took a half page advertisement in 'The Stage' announcing that Kathy had appointed me as her manager. That was on Thursday April 21st 1983, and my telephone never stopped ringing that day.

By this time I was fully aware of Kathy's fluctuating mood changes, and the times when she didn't appear to be entirely rational. However, I suppose in those early days, still with stars in my eyes, I only really saw what I wanted to see. Maybe I should have read what Ambrose had told the Sunday Express, way back in the sixties. For evidently the signs were there to be seen, 'She comes home from a show and sits in the chair until seven or eight in the morning, and talks the biggest load of balderdash you've ever heard. She's not what I would call normal for twenty-four hours after a show. It takes her a couple of days before she gets back into her stride again. I tell you," he went on. "I'm worried about the accumulation of all this mental disturbance on her health. It's frightening. I think she should see a psychiatrist. I've tried to fathom her out, but just can't."

The first bookings that came out were in May. On Thursday 19th, she appeared in two different venues. One was a restaurant in Walsall, and two hours later a similar establishment in Worcester. Both places sold out. The following night she appeared at the Prestbury Suite in Cheltenham. The Daily Mirror's sister paper in Scotland, The Daily Record, sent a reporter and photographer to cover Kathy's act and it would lead to a double page centre colour spread a few days later.

Inevitably, while going over all the old troubles of the past, the reporter wrote a sympathetic piece:-

"She began to sing and an extraordinary thing happened. The curiosity died and instead the room filled with emotion. They were listening to the sound of suffering, the voice of bruised humanity. For Kathy Kirby was the woman who embraced calamity like a lover. With every line of her songs she called up the calamities of her life."

In the audience that night, as he had been at all the other shows since I had first met him at Andreas' restaurant, was Kathy's latest boyfriend. His name was Alan Porter. A dark skinned, quiet man, who gave his occupation as being 'involved in politics'. I never did warm to him. He was currently working in Birmingham, and often Kathy would pop on a train from London to spend a weekend with him. She seemed happy with him, and would tell the Press that the new man in her life, as so often before, 'reminded her of Ambrose'. Unfortunately, with Alan working away from London for so much of the time, Kathy alone, would start telephoning me *at all times of the day or night, when she needed someone to talk with. Sometimes at three or four in the morning. Still, I thought, it was a small price to pay if I could get her career moving once more.*

IV

By this time in her life, she didn't really enjoy talking to the Press, and who could blame he?. It was always the same old questions they wanted to pick over; the bankruptcy, the domestic incidents, and the spell in the mental home. Usually said, 'thanks, but no thanks', when any telephone calls came requesting an interview. Although, of course, I realised that at this point the Press could have been useful.

The highly respected journalist Polly Toynbee, now with the BBC, but then writing her weekly page for The Guardian, telephoned and asked me if I could arrange a meeting. A quality newspaper with a serious journalist was, I thought, a different matter. I arranged to meet Miss Toynbee at Kathy's place in London on the 9th May. At first the interview seemed to go quite well, and as Polly remarked in her subsequent article.

"Considering what had gone before, I expected to see a defeated spectacle, a broken woman, But in she bounced, full of exotic, dizzy exuberance, unstoppable, effervescent talk. I could see what the judge meant about the problems of getting a straight answer. She bubbles, enthuses and talks about what she wants to talk about. She still talks like a star at the height of her career. Her dismal surroundings seem not to penetrate the hazy look in her eyes. There is something touchingly brave about it all."

The interview continued with Miss Toynbee, seemingly handling Kathy quite well, but as she observed:

"I mentioned other incidents in her life, and she became increasingly hard to follow, until suddenly she exploded with rage and fury. "I don't have to talk to you. I'm calling my lawyer. You're not to print a word."

Where it came from, or what it was all about was a mystery. Her manager tried to calm her down, and she turned on him, "you're fired. I don't want your contracts. Take them all away, I don't have to have anything to do with you, if I don't want to." The Guardian photographer was half smiling with embarrassment, and had long since stopped photographing her. "Take that smile off your face," she yelled. Her manager got angry too, and started answering her back. The photographer and I got out quick, not unmindful of the stories of others who had left with black eyes and tufts of hair missing. Good for her, I thought, once safely out on the street. It may not be the best way to handle the Press, when making a comeback in show business, but there's a lot to be said for not going gentle into that goodnight."

When Polly Toynbee and the photographer had gone, I just sat in the room and let Kathy rave on. Like Miss Toynbee, I had no idea either what had caused it, or where it had come from. In the end I just left with Kathy shouting abuse at me. I travelled home to Birmingham very depressed. Late into the night Kathy telephoned, she was perfectly normal and didn't mention the outburst earlier. She had just telephoned to make sure I had arrived home safely.

V

Putting all my doubts on one side, I had arranged a busy few weeks for Kathy. Following a radio interview on BBC Radio London, she was to appear, two days later in a programme for Channel 4 called, "Do You Remember?" It was an all star benefit gala for the stricken DJ, Stuart Henry. With Bob Barter leading the orchestra, she sang 'Secret Love' and won one of the biggest ovations of the evening.

The day before the concert I had agreed an appearance for her on TV AM, with the show's official bill topper, American, Del Shannon, to plug the concert. The car collected her at 6.30am for her 7 o'clock call, which didn't please her too much. Indeed, it really did seem evident, judging from this latest TV appearance, that she could not answer a simple question directly. Asked by the interviewer if 'she had any problems breaking away from singing 'Secret Love'?, Kathy pulled the question apart, dissecting it and eventually asked the young woman what she meant. "I do an hour's spot, a complete act of which 'Secret Love' is just one song."

I gave up and went and took a shower.

I booked her for a cabaret appearance at 'Rockshots' in Newcastle-Upon-Tyne for Friday June 3rd. I was unable to attend as I had a long-standing contract at the Civic Centre, Chelmsford that week. I telephoned Bob Barter, her musical director, at the hotel where they were staying, and was told the venue had been very pleased with Kathy's work. To make the long trip more attractive, the following night I arranged a cabaret at the Cascade Club in Winsford, Cheshire. It would only mean a small detour on the journey back down to London and the offered fee was good.

The headlines in the following Monday's newspapers gave a full account of Kathy's behaviour, and was something, both she, and I, could have done without. That day my telephone never stopped ringing. Calls from future bookers needing my assurance that Kathy's forthcoming appearance at their venue was definite. In Winsford it seems, Kathy had sat weeping in Bob's car, claiming that she was too ill to go on stage that night. The crowd, disappointed with her non-appearance spotted her huddled in the car park at the back of the club, and started to yell obscenities. A doctor was called and after examining her told the club officials that "she was just being silly". It was rather ironic in the end that Bob Barter should entertain the crowd in the club for over an hour, playing his organ, trying to placate them, in which time Kathy could have done her spot and the two of them could have been heading down the motorway with another good fee in her pocket. With headlines like: "Fans Rage At Kathy", alarm bells had begun to sound in my head. However, for the time being, I would persevere.

The company that booked Kathy into the Cascade Club threatened to sue me for her non-appearance that night. It was the first, and not the last time, I had to consult my solicitor regarding Kathy's behaviour

The letter read: " Thank you for attending our offices on June 10th and we note your problems with regard to the above.

The position as we see it is that you, in your capacity as manager for Kathy Kirby arranged a booking at the Cascade Social Club for her, through JAM Productions on June 4th last.

We take the view that, prima facie, there is no agency relationship, though we do concede that a court may find that you were her agent.

It is clear from the information that you have given us that Kathy Kirby was in flagrant breach of her contract, and as such, you are not legally liable, though you will appreciate that the information we have received has been very brief indeed.

At present JAM Productions are claiming compensation from you in the sum of £150 and it appears that this does not represent a true measure of their loss, in view of the fact that as a result of the incident at the Cascade Social Club, perhaps other associate clubs will no longer deal with them. In the circumstances, and in view of your correct intention that this is not a matter in which you wish to become involved, we suggest that a payment be made to JAM without an admission of liability and on condition that a receipt issued stating that such a payment is made in full and final settlement.

We note that you do not wish to become involved in proceedings and would advise that if JAM seek legal advice, a far greater claim may be made and the onus will then be up to you to bring Miss Kirby into such proceedings, which could very costly and distressing.......Yours faithfully, Garrett and Co.

Two weeks later she was at the Majestic Recording Studios in southwest London, to pre-record her two numbers for Channel 4's 'Unforgettable' series, which was introduced each week by Alan Freeman. The following day, 14th June, she drove down to Sinatra's Club in Croydon to film the show, with Bob Barter ever at her side. Although she looked lovely when the show was finally broadcast, now knowing her moods so well, I realised from the performance, she wasn't in the best of moods. All became clear when I later learnt that at the club, she had a terrible argument with her boyfriend, Alan, just before filming her first spot. Her second appearance, singing 'Let Me Go Lover', then had to be shot several times, as Kathy was not happy with the finished result. Certainly the immaculate hairstyle with which she greeted viewers in the first half of the show, didn't bear any resemblance to the style they saw after 'Lover' had been filmed to Kathy's satisfaction.

Barrie Stacey telephoned me and asked if Kathy would be prepared to top the bill at a charity event he was organising at Hornsea Town Hall. The Gala was on behalf of CATS, The Children's Aid Team for mentally handicapped children. The organisation had been founded some eight years earlier by an old friend of Kathy's, Lena David. Lena had, of course, written the song, 'Singer In The Band', for Kathy, as a tribute to her time with Ambrose. The charity's chief aim was to help the mentally handicapped and their families in the community. Kathy had always been very fond of Miss Davis and jumped at the opportunity to appear.

The show was held on Tuesday June 28th, and I travelled to London to escort Kathy to Hornsea. With her smiling photograph on the cover of the souvenir programme, although the official bill topper, she elected to close the first half. Others on the bill included the international jazz star, Adelaide Hall, the vocalist, Carl Wayne, and the Music Hall comedian, George Williams.

The Gala was a sell out, with Kathy seemingly being the chief attraction. Now considered almost as infamous as famous, she was acquiring something of a legendary reputation in the business. Her personal life had been the subject of scores of headlines for years, and audiences were now arriving to watch this woman, wondering how she survived it all.

As The Stage newspaper reported, "but it was Kathy Kirby who caused tremendous excitement with her set of the evening. Looking and sounding the Superstar she is, she breezed through her old hits and threw in a powerful performance of 'Maybe This Time', only topping that with 'My Yiddishe Momma'. It seems that this year will be a good one for Kirby, now currently on tour."

Surrounded by her fans in the interval, she was happy that night. Barrie Stacey had arranged for a car to take her back to the flat in southwest London that she had recently moved to, and there we had a bottle of wine, before I set off for Euston to catch the train home. Seeing her perform so well that night, and winning the kind of ovation I always felt she deserved, I could forgive her anything. Any doubts I had were forgotten.

I was very selective with the bookings I took for Kathy, not wanting to push her too hard. Certainly the telephone hardly stopped ringing in my home, with offers of work during that summer of 1983. She did engagements in Manchester and Cumbria, and was part of an all star sixties night at Butlins, staged at their Barry Island holiday centre. Attending that night, it was certainly true, when the critic from The Stage reported that 'Kathy Kirby was moved to tears at the end of her act by her reception from the crowd.'

The erratic telephone calls, both night and day, were beginning to get me down. But I was still determined to continue getting her career back on track. Kirby fans often telephoned as well, to say how delighted they were to see Kathy around again, working so well, on both stage and television. She was in the news again, but favourably for once.

Appearing at the Patti Pavilion in Swansea, during the summer, Lee Wilson telephoned me from the offices of The Mail on Sunday. Although mindful of what happened with Polly Toynbee a few months earlier, I arranged for him to see Kathy before a show, and review her performance.

He wrote a superb piece, and gave the following review of her concert.

"They broke into cheers when Miss Kirby swept onto the stage.

She was nearly half an hour late in appearing, and a few of her fans were getting anxious about catching their buses. But when Miss Kirby began to belt out 'Maybe This Time', they sat rooted to the edge of their seats. It was a hypnotic performance. The voice has the same astonishing range, and almost too much power. But it wasn't the sound so much as the presence, which kept the audience's eyes fixed on her. She didn't appear to have grown old, as other pop singer's have grown old. She seemed unchanged, as if all the in-between times had been a mask, which she could slip off. On stage all the doubt and self-agonising disappears. I asked her if she had created an image for herself, since so many other people seemed to have created their own Kathy Kirby versions. She didn't seem to understand the question. She didn't know who she was. But watching her, the enigma becomes clearer. She is a performer. At the end of her act, she took four curtain calls, and one by one the audience stood up enthusiastically clapping and calling for more."

Kathy made a further television appearance that year, as one of the guests on 'This Is Your Life'. The subject was the disc jockey, Stuart Henry, for who Kathy had appeared on 'Do You Remember?' earlier in the year. President Records re-released her old Decca album, 'Kathy Kirby sings 16 hits from Stars and Garters', in a new sleeve, under the title of

'Let Me Sing And I'm Happy', and Kathy was looking forward to ending the year topping the bill in a short Christmas season in cabaret in Blackpool.

I was happy with what I had achieved in 1983. Little did I know it was soon to be the beginning of the end of our working relationship. Like everyone else, I would turn my back on her and walk away.   *JH*

Chapter Thirteen

Walk Away

"I'm not a masochist you know. I'm straining my vocal chords for you."

Kathy Kirby

I

Very pleased with the way things had gone, I took another large advertisement out in The Stage, with the genuine reviews that Kathy had earned over the past few months. The response was very good and the 1984 diary was quickly filling up.

I had long been booked to appear in pantomime that Christmas, with Jim Bowen in Aladdin, at the Pavilion Theatre, Weymouth, and couldn't really get out of it. So, before my own rehearsals began, I travelled up to Blackpool to sort out Kathy's accommodation in the resort, for her and Alan Porter, for the run of the show. I found it very difficult obtaining a flat for her, as many places were already fully booked for over the festive season. However, after about six hours of walking the streets, I eventually found a suitable place. Unfortunately, the two of them would have to book into a hotel for the final evening of the run, as the proprietor had it booked for the last night. Holiday flats being booked from Saturday to Saturday.

Barrie Stacey's 'Christmas Spectacular', opened a three-week season on December 19th, at the Horseshoe Showbar, on the south shore, with a different star name topping the bill each week. Kathy opened the season and was to be followed by singer Ruby Murray, and then Elizabeth Dawn, better known to viewers of Coronation Street as Vera Duckworth. The supporting bill included comedian, George Williams and the instrumental speciality act, Linda Grant.

Arriving with a cold, the eventual review in the Stage would state, "Kathy Kirby fought against a throat complaint on her opening night, and lost!" Worse was to come though. During my run at Weymouth, I received the following letter from Barrie Stacey's company manager in Blackpool. It read:

Dear James,

Please find enclosed copies of letters to Miss Kirby, a doctor's certificate, and my letter to Barrie Stacey, with a breakdown of Miss Kirby's salary.

As stated on the telephone this afternoon, it would have been better if Miss Kirby had been honest with Barrie from the beginning and said she was unable to perform for the week.

As it was, she was on stage for twenty-two minutes on Monday, fifteen minutes Tuesday, and less on Wednesday, as well as insulting the audience. We cancelled the show on Thursday as we were unable to find a replacement singer, which caused unpleasantness from the Horseshoe Showbar, and managed to find a girl singer for Friday's show, for which she was paid £80.

To top it all, on Saturday morning when Miss Kirby had to leave the accommodation, and I found her a hotel for the day, she had a screaming row with her boyfriend, and then accused the hotel housekeeper of assaulting her. What more can I say?

On behalf of Barrie Stacey Promotions.

Her missed performances made headlines in both the local newspaper in Blackpool, and more importantly The Stage. Being stuck in Weymouth there was little I could do. Perhaps it was fortunate I did not know there was much worse to come, during the first week of the New Year.

London Weekend Television were presenting a new series called 'Knees Up', hosted by cockney comedian Jeff Stevenson. It was set in a pub, and the atmosphere was reminiscent of the old days of 'Stars and Garters'. Extras were drafted in to become the customers, sitting around the bar area, tables and chairs, they would watch the floorshow. The programme featured a couple of different star guests each week. Teresa Brewer, the American songstress, was the chief attraction on the first show, and I duly booked Kathy for the star spot on the second. It was an important booking for her, as it went out at prime time on a Sunday evening.

I arranged with the musical director, Mike Alexander, what two numbers Kathy would sing and we agreed on 'Maybe This Time' and 'Let Me Go Lover'. Mike then did the arrangements for the thirteen-piece orchestra. A car was arranged to collect Kathy from her flat on Friday January 6th, to record the show for airing the following Sunday. Not being able to go myself, due to my Weymouth commitments, I received a telephone call at the theatre from London Weekend. Kathy had sent the chauffeur driven car away, informing the driver that she didn't feel like doing the show that particular day. I just couldn't believe it. A later call received from the company informed me that the studios were considering legal action, and that the Head of Light Entertainment, David Bell, would make sure that Kathy never worked for them ever again. What was the point of going on? Did Kathy have no understanding of the opportunity she had just blown? Totally depressed, I eventually completed my season at Weymouth and returned home. Refusing to take her calls, I felt all the hard work I had done was being eroded by her actions. I might as well call it a day. I had yet to receive a penny in commission, however, that was far from the front of my mind. I was just so angry with her. How could she behave like that and throw it all away?

With a great deal of work in the book for the New Year, I had intended to start making deductions for my commission. But now I was writing to the various promoters saying that I no longer represented her and that I couldn't be held responsible for her actions, or non-completion of her contracts.

One by one the offers of work were withdrawn. A major London appearance at the Beck Theatre, Hillingdon, in February; Sunday concerts during the summer; headlining in the Isle of Man, and a five week season in cabaret throughout May and June in Jersey, earning the kind of money she hadn't seen offered in years... and so on.

Eventually I took her call, and sadly, perhaps the most pathetic part was she could not really understand why I had withdrawn my services. She continued to telephone after I resigned, but by then I didn't really want to know. She has not worked in any medium since.

Chapter Fourteen

Let Me Go Lover

"James, I'm not myself, I'm not the real Kathy Kirby."
Kathy Kirby

I

*The questions of Kathy Kirby's life. Her relationship with
Ambrose and her career, are legion. I'm not really sure how
well I actually got to know her. For me she was two people;
the kind, softly spoken woman, caring, with a fantastic memory
and who had one of the sharpest minds I had ever known,
then the erratic troubled soul whose conversations made no
sense. So often a delight to speak to and then suddenly
becoming a totally different person. A very difficult scenario
for anyone to cope with.*

*How do you answer the star when she asks, in all
seriousness; "Where is the real Kathy Kirby?" I have many
messages left on my answerphone by her, which confirms, at
least to me, that she does indeed need professional help. Once,
when I rang her to see if she'd like to appear on Central TV,
her reply was "how could I work at present when I don't have
my own voice or body."*

As I mentioned earlier, Ambrose told the Press of the rubbish she would talk after a stage show. Was the problem always there? Certainly Ambrose dominated Kathy; he thought for her, told her what to sing, how to dress and make-up, but did he ignore the rest? Or was he part of the trouble? Is his legacy to her the woman she is now? All that can be accurately said, although their relationship was stormy and tempestuous, he seemed to be the only one who could handle her and the rewards of their partnership can simply be measured by the success she achieved.

Kathy's mother, Eileen, used to telephone me occasionally, having met me a few times at concert dates. A highly-strung woman, her relationship with the singer was equally explosive. She died a few years ago. During one telephone conversation with Kathy, she told me that her mother had committed suicide. I don't know if this turned out to be true or not. Certainly it failed to make the newspapers, but then again why should it?

In the end I could not cope anymore with the endless telephone calls, with Kathy talking of things, no rational person could understand. I recorded a couple of these, as I didn't actually believe what I was hearing. They make painful listening today. I could transcribe them here, but it would serve no real purpose, and in the end I have too much respect for the artiste to do so. As Eileen Kirby once said; "My daughter is a very sick girl, she does need help."

I don't know why that treatment was never forthcoming by either her family or close friends. Perhaps, like me, they became worn out by the calls, the split personality and the temperamental behaviour, that they turned a blind eye, and left it for someone else to deal with. So far no one has.

II

My telephone would still ring asking for Kathy's services. I no longer gave any agents or promoters her home number, as the singer told me off in no uncertain terms the last time I did. I simply stated that she was not working at present. Fan letters were still directed to me, from the The Stage etc., with requests of signed photographs and asking why she was not heard of much these days. A couple of recently released compact discs of her years with Decca and EMI have increased my postbag, and young people are discovering her, wanting details of her recording career and biographies. Each letter asking the same question; "Why isn't she working?"

It made me very depressed that she wasn't. As Don Phillips once remarked. "What she needs is another Ambrose." The likelihood of that happening must be very remote. So many people who believed in her talent, who, if they couldn't actually fit completely into Ambrose's shoes, have all fallen by the wayside. Could we all have been wrong?

Some years ago, when I thought I was writing the final section of this book I wrote:-

I last saw Kathy a couple of years ago. I bumped into her purely by chance on Birmingham's New Street Station. She had been in town for the weekend to visit Alan Porter, and was now waiting for the same train back to London. She looked just the same as ever, a little fuller in the figure perhaps, but the magic still showed in her face. We travelled to London together and parted company at Euston Station. I promised I would call her soon, I never did, I loved her, but couldn't get back aboard that crazy merry-go-round again.

Soon after, returning from a busy panto season, I found a special Christmas card waiting for me. The message just said, "To James, with love, Kathy". I felt slightly guilty that I hadn't sent her a festive card, and I picked up the telephone in my flat maybe a dozen times that morning, half dialling her London number. It would be nice to hear that unmistakeable voice, to hear how she was keeping. In the end though, I decided against it.

The previous Saturday evening, December 21st, BBC2 had televised the original 1964 edition of 'Christmas Night With The Stars'. Having set the video to record the show, I sat back that morning to watch the programme. Following appearances by Benny Hill, Dick Emery, Billy Cotton's Bandshow and short festive editions of the popular 'Likely Lads' and 'The Marriage Lines', Jack Warner introduced the top of the bill, Miss Kathy Kirby. Like a dream walking, her pure, crystal voice offered the viewers, 'Have Yourself A Merry Little Christmas'. Looking at the old black and white picture, I thought of all that had happened to her since the programme. I could see why so often, at the height of her fame, she was referred to as this country's answer to Marilyn Monroe. A compliment, maybe, but for me she was Great Britain's Kathy Kirby, and I needed or wanted no more than that.

Very little of Kathy remains on film, from the height of her fame in the sixties. BBC2 ran a three show series devoted to the archives and over the weeks Cilla Black, Dusty Springfield and Lulu all had their moments of glory. Scores of letters were sent to Television Centre, and the 'Points Of View' programme, asking just one question, 'why was no Kathy Kirby show included in the series?' The presenter was Anne Robinson, who was forced to explain that no show now exists. All have been wiped clean. Such was the outcry, that the following week the programmed showed a clip of Kathy at the height of her powers, singing 'Secret Love' on the Royal Variety Performance 1964.

Small consolation indeed.

***Telling what I thought was the story of the end of my
relationship with Kathy I wrote:-***

*The last time I contacted Kathy was in February 1993,
much against my better judgement. I was on tour with the
Willie Russell musical, 'Our Day Out', working for my close
friend, Alexander (Peter) Bridge.*

*One day, during a week at the Alexandra Theatre in
Bognor, I got onto the subject of Kathy. Although not himself
a fan of the singer, Peter had witnessed her great success at
Hornsea some years earlier, and thought her ripe for a
comeback. He was keen to present her. We discussed the
possibility and I duly wrote to Kathy with details of the offer.*

*Peter thought she would still be big box office, and made
a pencil booking for a Sunday concert at the beautiful
Wimbledon Theatre, that October. With a strong supporting
bill, he also instructed his musical director to score a long
overture, comprising of the songs most associated with Kathy,
to give her a prolonged build-up before her entrance. Made
in an emotional style as Judy Garland's had been during her
final concert years. I contacted the journalist and broadcaster,
Derek Jameson, regarding the possibility of him introducing
her, knowing him to be a big Kirby fan; he readily agreed.*

All looked set for a major comeback, with Peter stating

that should the show go well, he would want to present Kathy at major theatres around the country. It was left to Kathy to respond. She rejected my letter, and the offer, out of hand and said,. "How can I work at the moment when I don't even have my own feet?"

Is that all there is? Born in 1938, she is still a comparatively young woman. Maybe she will confound us all and make that big comeback. I wish her all the luck in the world, and would travel from the other side of the world to applaud her entrance. She is, after all, my favourite singer.

Old fading reviews and newspaper clippings place on record the colossal impact she made; and the recordings preserve the pure magic of her voice....but, to think, what might have been.

There was indeed to be more.

Chapter Fifteen

So Here I Go (Again)!

"James it's Kathy, I need your help."
Kathy Kirby

I

Much against my better judgement I once again boarded the merry-go-round in 1996. In October of the previous year a play by Jimmy Chinn entitled 'Whatever Happened To Kathy Kirby?', was presented by the highly respected non-professional theatre company The New Stagers Theatre Club in Wandsworth, South East London. The company were then into their thirty-eighth year of providing quality drama for the local community; and this particular production was no exception, achieving rave reviews and house full performances.

Unfortunately, while the play was indeed a fine drama, the very title of the piece was misleading for it certainly didn't answer the question it was asking in its title. The action centred around a young man who had an obsession with the blonde singing star – the storyline and drama being heightened at regular intervals with excerpts of Kathy's recordings.

Kathy had heard about the production and was not very happy

that her name was being used in a production that had no relevance to her own life story, and was being produced without first seeking her permission. Out of the blue she rang me to voice her concerns. During a lengthy telephone call she explained it all to me. I told her that I would be in London during the next couple of weeks on business and would make arrangements to visit her at her flat to discuss it all.

One week later I found myself back in her company visiting her along with my agent Tony Hyland and a close friend the highly respected comedian Dave Peters. Yorkshire based Dave was at that time playing a season at the world famous Players Theatre underneath The Arches in Villiers Street, where its reputation had become legendary. Dave was keen to meet another legend.

Kathy greeted the three of us warmly and I noticed immediately a stark contrast to the last time I had seen her. More serene and quiet, there was an inner calmness there that I had never witnessed before.

Always the generous hostess, we had a few glasses of wine with her and the four of us discussed everything from the play in question to swapping our own show business stories. Dave has a wealth of reminiscences and Kathy found him highly amusing. When we eventually left nothing had been said of our past disputes and I gave her a promise I would look into the production of 'Whatever Happened To Kathy Kirby?'

I discovered that the play had been performed by several other companies in the Greater London area. Kathy's life long fan David Innes told me of his visit to a venue in Richmond, Surrey to see the show, intrigued by the title of the piece. I remember he told me that the run had been extended by several weeks – but again not taking anything away from the critically acclaimed piece – how much was the fabulous business at the box office due to having the singer's name in its title?

I eventually spoke to the author, Jimmy Chinn, at length on the telephone. It was apparent during these conversations that he was a great admirer of the star. Explaining Kathy's reservations and objections, the gentleman that he is, he agreed to make some major changes to the play. These are best described by quoting from a letter I had at a much later date from the director of the production, Peter W. Brooker:

"I understand that because of various objections raised by Kathy Kirby the production had to be scrapped. The play has since been re-titled and re-written. No mention of her remains in the published script and none

of her recordings are featured. The author has substituted the name of a fictional singer and because of that, in my opinion, the play no longer has the same emotional charge. It is such a shame that Miss Kirby felt unable, for whatever reasons, to allow the production to go ahead as originally written. I am certain that had it gone ahead it would have led to renewed interest in her career and gained her a whole new generation of fans. Perhaps though, that is exactly what she did not want to happen. You are obviously a better judge of that than I am.

Our production was a great success and is still talked about with much affection by those involved. It gained Miss Kirby a great many new fans from among the drama group that presented it – most of whom weren't even born at the time of her greatest successes."

Job accomplished, Kathy was very pleased and I once more boarded the merry-go-round. Fortunately, now though it was moving at a much more sedate pace.

II

With Kathy still turning down all offers of work – they hadn't actually stopped during the period we weren't actually in touch –

I had what I thought was a brainwave as I approached my '97/'98 pantomime season at the Royal Tunbridge Wells. That year I was playing Widow Twankey to John Leslie's Aladdin in the pantomime of the same name. I thought it would be nice to buy Kathy some really expensive Christmas presents that year with the help and contributions from her fans. For example, up to this point she had never owned her own video recorder. The aforementioned David Innes had previously released (under license from the BBC) a superb CD "Kathy Kirby – The Long Lost Shows". These were recordings taken from her BBC Television shows that David had painstakingly digitally remastered and restored from his original recordings. Many hours of work were involved but the finished result and CD was and is breathtaking in its quality. Selling it privately by mail order from advertisements placed in all the trade magazines, David had built up a list of Kirby admirers who had purchased the CD. With him kindly letting me have a copy of all the people who had bought the recording, I did a circular letter to all the addresses I had been provided with stating my wish to get Kathy some really nice Christmas presents that year. Upon receipt of a donation of £10 or more towards the gifts, I would guarantee a personally signed photograph to them from Kathy once my pantomime season had finished in mid-January.

The cheques came flooding in, some fans sending in as much as £50. Unfortunately some helpful person also tipped off The Stage newspaper about my intentions and they published a large piece together with the fact that I was appearing at The Assembly Halls Theatre over the Christmas period. The cheques also then started to arrive at the theatre. They were obviously very welcome but I was very annoyed about the unwanted publicity.

I recall I raised around £800 and was able to buy much more than I originally envisaged: a colour television for her bedroom, the aforementioned video recorder, a top of the range music centre, a CD player and a number of smaller gifts such as a new clock radio for her bedside cabinet. Unfortunately, so much generosity and the number of items caused its own problems!

Kathy lives in a quiet cul-de-sac in South London. The spacious flat is near the top of a converted massive Victorian building, with the only approach being up a virtually 'spiral' wooden staircase. There would be no way I would be able to carry all the presents up to her apartment on my own. So who would I ask knowing how much she protects her privacy? Unfortunately, the obvious choice Tony, my agent, who she had met on previous occasions was currently away on business in America.

Ever since the Hornsea Town Hall Gala, I had kept in touch with a very affable Kirby fan from Kent. His name was John. With my pantomime rehearsals fast approaching I needed to get the gifts to Kathy as quickly as possible. She of course still being totally unaware at this point of the collection I had made. I simply told her that I had a couple of items for her that I could not manage on my own and would have to get someone to help me carry them up to her place. I virtually gave her no choice. I asked John if he would help me. He obviously jumped at the chance as Kathy had long been his favourite singer.

Umpteen journeys up and down those bloody stairs, Kathy was amazed by all the boxes John and I carried in. She was also very gracious to John while he reminded me of myself all those years ago on that fateful evening at that club in Southampton where I first met her. Open mouthed comes to mind!

Kathy was a little cross with me when I told her about the collection but secretly I could tell she was very pleased with all the gifts. In the New Year after my season had finished she happily signed individual letters of thanks and photographs to all the generous people that had taken part. Something very special though happened that Christmas beyond the presents and all the eagerly anticipated photographs that went in the post.

John proved to have been a wise choice in getting him to help me that day. For the last eight years he has proved himself to have been a good, loyal and totally dependable friend to Kathy. Holding down a full time job yet somehow always being there for her – day or night – whenever he is needed. To pinch someone else's analogy, he really has become her rock.

Thank you John, so much.

III

The offers of work still come in on a regular basis. Anything from a major television appearance to interviews on both national and local radio stations. Just recently two local BBC radio stations had to settle for me to talk about the Kirby phenomenon such is the interest she still generates. It seems that for over forty years now her audience has never wavered in its loyalty.

I appreciate that some people in the media feel I keep her too protected from outside pressures and sources. However, I am only following her wishes. I realise that it can be hard to understand how Kathy can turn down many exciting offers – indeed the television programme makers and national tabloid reporters can be both indignant and persistent when a thank you but no thank you is offered to the latest contract on the table before her. They can't actually understand how Kathy isn't interested in appearing in a major television show or not agree to a double page interview for a national newspaper. I suppose though it is unusual. Unwittingly though by keeping out of the spotlight she is only enhancing the myth and icon status that now surrounds her. Frequently she is now referred to in the popular Press as 'The Garbo of Pop'.

In the Spring of 2004 I took a telephone call from a company called L.A. Productions – a film and television production company who were based in Liverpool. Probably one of their best-known productions is the award winning film 'Letter To Brezhnev'. It transpired that the company were very interested in filming the life story of Kathy for television. I travelled to Liverpool to meet the producer Colin McKeown and at a later date to London to meet the projects leading lady who was desperate to play (and meet) Kathy: Amanda Holden. She was quite charming. I caught her in her West End debut show a few weeks later where she was starring in 'Thoroughly Modern Millie' at the Shaftesbury Theatre. Miss Holden was excellent, though I left in the interval not thinking much of the show. A poor book and only the title song being one of any note. But then what do I know?

Explaining all the details to Kathy, she gave her written consent and blessings for the projection to go ahead however refused all meeting with either Miss Holden, Mr McKeown or anyone else from the production team. She made it clear all questions and queries should be asked via me. I don't think that they were too happy about this (which I can fully understand) but it is simply the way it is. Hopefully one day the project will get off the ground.

Also early in 2004 I was contacted by a journalist with the respected Sunday Express. They had discovered that Kathy's niece and god-daughter Claudia (the daughter of Kathy's sister Pat and her husband Terry) had married the owner of the Mail Newspaper Group, Jonathan Harmsworth – the current Lord Rothermere. With a circulation war on going between the Express and Mail organisations, this fact could prove to be a very tasty titbit they had uncovered. The newspaper was prepared to pay mega bucks for Kathy's reaction. Particularly as Kathy's two other nieces (from her sister Pat) had both married into aristocratic families: the youngest daughter, Katya tied the knot to the Baronet Heir Richard Pilkington and in 1996 the eldest daughter Sarah had wed Lord Francis Hastings Russell, a chartered surveyor.

Kathy did not receive one wedding invitation.

I travelled to London to meet the journalists at their Ludgate House office. Keen to get Kathy's reaction, they couldn't have been more accommodating with their offer. They didn't feel it was essential to meet with Kathy, leaving it with me to ask her the few simple questions they wanted her response and reaction to. It was explained to me that Kathy's brother-in-law Terry Clemence from owning a second-hand car dealership in Essex was now a multi-millionaire living with Pat in a five million pound house in exclusive Belgravia, a short drive from Kathy's own home. Where had the money come from?

In the sixties Pat had tried for a singing career like her more famous sister and actually released a couple of single recordings. She never emulated Kathy's success or fame however, failing to reach the heights Kathy achieved, she eventually sought and had a relatively successful career in modelling in the fashion industry. What is ironic though is that at the height of her fame Kathy often picked up the tab for anything that her sister and brother-in-law wanted while they were sharing in the heady days of her astonishing success. Now forty years on, Kathy didn't even have a telephone number or an address for them. Yet they were living a life of wealth and privilege so close to where she resided. What is so sad is that they know exactly where Kathy does live because she would always receive greetings cards at Christmas and on her birthday. Only they know why they haven't been in touch, made any proper contact and arranged to meet.

I wonder what Lord Rothermere would have made of the fact that I was contacted in 2000 by a senior reporter from the Daily Mail requesting an interview with Kathy for a full feature on her life and career. The same lady who both his, and his wife's family have so pointedly ignored in all these years.

The fax read:-

'I am writing to say how much we would love to interview Kathy Kirby for a full feature in the Daily Mail.

I am sure she is constantly busy, so apologies in advance for adding this to the pile. We would, however, very much welcome the opportunity to talk about her remarkable life and career, her outstanding successes as one of the major singing stars of the Sixties and her recollections of that era, as well as any of her current projects and hopes and plans for the future.

The interview, which could be done at any time or place convenient to her, would be conducted by one of our most senior feature writers and would take no longer than one and a half hours of her time. Naturally we would be more than happy to tie in the interview with anything she is currently involved in and to provide a full credit within the piece.

I would be most grateful if you could contact me to let me know if anything can be arranged-if at all possible, this week. In the meantime thank you very much for your time and consideration.

Yours sincerely,

Fiona McPhillips, Associate Features Editor.'

Similar circumstances surround Douglas, Kathy's brother who she adored. A very successful businessman in Essex, he too keeps in touch with similar greetings cards but again she has not actually seen him in many years. All she has is a telephone number of the workplace of her nephew Paul, Douglas' son that she can use in an emergency to get a message to her brother. The saddest aspect of all this is that I have never heard her say one unkind word about either her brother or sister.

During the period of her life when she was constantly moving from one home to another on a regular basis, Kathy left an awful lot of her own possessions in storage at her mother, Eileen's home in Jason Close in Brentwood, Essex. These included the remaining jewellery that the bailiffs didn't take, a couple of stunning oil paintings which she sat for at the height of her fame and a filing cabinet stuffed with her music, photographs and the negatives and a host of personal papers and letters which were irreplaceable. Nothing was ever returned to her. After Eileen's death the house was emptied and Douglas didn't inform Kathy of the date of her mother's funeral until after it had taken place in case her presence attracted any unwanted publicity.

I left the Express office and travelled over to see Kathy with the fabulous offer that was being dangled. Ever the lady, although she was tempted by the amount of money involved (and heaven knows it would have been life changing for her) she didn't feel it was proper to talk to the Press about her family. Both John and I thought she was crazy – these were the same people that had ignored her for the past thirty years never once coming to her aid during all the problems she had gone through and somehow surviving on her own. It didn't help that her old boyfriend Alan Porter, crept out of the woodwork and advised her not to co-operate with the newspaper. He too hadn't seen Kathy in a number of years having settled in Birmingham in the early 1980s. He did ring her however from time to time to see how she was. I told Kathy it would be more helpful when he offered her advice if he was in possession of the full facts and if he rang me, I would give them to him. He never did of course, and Kathy was not able to give me his number so I could call him as he would always withhold his own number when he called her from Birmingham. That says it all about him, I feel.

I left Kathy with the thought that I had been advised that the newspaper would be going ahead with the article with or without her co-operation. The full-page spread eventually appeared on Sunday 28th March 2004. The headline screamed: "The British Monroe, the Rich Family who Abandoned her, and the Daily Mail

Lord's wife." Upon seeing it Kathy simply stated; "I should have listened to you and John".

One can only offer conjecture why her family has neglected her for so many years. Certainly during her bankruptcy she named Terry Clemence as one of the people responsible for her financial discrepancies. After the death of Ambrose, Terry acted as her financial adviser and they opened a joint bank account with the Midland Bank in Chadwell Heath in Essex. The account was to be used for business and personal expenditure. Kathy claims that it was only after her original creditors meeting that she discovered that Terry had drawn cheques on the account for his own purposes and none of the said cheques had included her own signature. Over £30,000 went from the account, Kathy alleges.

Whatever the truth, this and so many other chapters in her life explain why she now trusts so very few people. I remember after the successful Patti Pavilion concert in Swansea way back in 1983, she was chatting to the reporter from The Mail on Sunday, Lee Wilson. I can't recall the question he asked her now at the very end of the interview, but I will never forget Kathy's reply. It closed Lee Wilson's article; "The trouble is, men love me so much they always end up taking all my money." She looked bleakly at the floor, "Oh dear," she said, "I don't think I've got anything left for people to take anymore."

In October 2002, on impulse, I wrote to the Cliff Richard

Charitable Trust detailing Kathy's (then) financial difficulties. Kathy had of course toured with Sir Cliff at the beginning of the swinging sixties and both had shared the heady excitement of the British music industry of that time. Writing was obviously a misjudgement on my part. This was the response I received from Bill Latham, who fulfils a number of functions for Sir Cliff, including acting as his manager, business adviser and religious consultant.

Dear Mr Harman,

Thank you for our letter of October 21st regarding Kathy Kirby.

I regret that we are unable to offer financial assistance. This Trust is authorised by the Charity Commissioners to donate only to UK registered charities and not, directly or indirectly, to individuals. Student grants, loans or sponsorships, or contributions to personal or business needs, are therefore not permissible.

I am sorry therefore that the Trust could not help Kathy financially, but, as I say, this kind of assistance does not fall within its terms of reference. We do wish Kathy all the very best, and I know that Sir Cliff, who is on tour now almost continuously until March, would want me to convey his own greetings and good wishes to her also.

Yours sincerely, Bill Latham

I was rather peeved! I understood what had been stated, but surely an exception could have been made? Sir Cliff must have been fully aware of the professional and personal problems that Kathy had faced since the death of Ambrose. The Press coverage had been virtually relentless during the seventies.

It didn't really seem in keeping with his own well-publicised Christian, compassionate beliefs. Surely a private gift from one fellow professional to another would have been possible? However that kind of action doesn't generate the kind of Press, coverage that, for example, offering a free holiday to Tony and Cherie Blair at his holiday retreat in Portugal produces in all the national newspapers.

I wrote a brief note back acknowledging the reply. I also mentioned that I would try to get in touch with Sir Paul McCartney, who had, spontaneously, been so generous to Kathy in the past. I didn't, but felt better for saying I would!

Today Cliff Richard's personal fortune is estimated at £40million.

IV

But back to today and still my telephone rings. Just recently she was asked to top the bill at a major venue in one of her favourite resorts – Blackpool. So convinced was the promoter of the business she would do he spoke to me about his wish to then bring it to the London Palladium for one night. I don't doubt Kathy would still sell out. A newly built website (which I oversee) designed by Graham Smith and Mike Muir – www.kathykirby.co.uk -is now her official site and attracts over 5,000 hits a day from all over the world, and this leads to one of the oddest stories of all in Kathy's rich and tempestuous life.

With the success of the last couple of CD releases, Kathy had been getting an awful lot of Press coverage in 2004 and 2005 with reviews of the recordings and several re-appraisals of the Kirby career. She was in the newspapers an awful lot again. It was then that I started to get emails sent to her website, all asking for the answer to the same question. "Is Kathy Kirby still alive then?" I was stunned, mystified and intrigued and went in search of answers.

I eventually discovered that a tombstone in Northwood Cemetery in Middlesex is inscribed with the words 'Kathy Kirby – Secret Love'. I simply couldn't believe it. It was most bizarre and I was determined to discover the truth behind the writing on this well tended and cared for grave.

Mother of three, Kathleen Dyer, died tragically young with cancer in 1986. Both she and her husband Jim (a retired BT worker now living in Bournemouth) were big fans of Kathy. "Secret Love" was their favourite song, which Jim used to sing to his wife and indeed his pet name for Kathleen was 'Kathy Kirby'. "Secret Love" was played at Kathleen's funeral service and Jim and his children felt that the inscription on the heart shaped tombstone would be totally fitting for his wife because of the history that they had shared.

Unfortunately, while a lovely story, it was also somewhat misleading. Cemetery workers often discovered members of the public – fans of the singer – leaving flowers at the grave convinced it was the star herself that they were playing tribute to. Upon investigation I was told there was no legal issue with the deceased real name not being on the tombstone as long as it was in the official register.

James Dyer plans to be buried in the same grave, next to his beloved wife and the tombstone will then have both their names added.

V

Kathy Kirby has known much joy and tragedy in her life. Lesser mortals would not have coped with all that life has thrown at her. Content, and now living a quiet life away from the spotlight, with all that she has gone through, I think we have to respect her privacy. Still justly famous for her superb voice and artistry, she is proof that genuine talent is not trapped in any one generation or time.

Some people who live difficult and tempestuous lives manage to endure and survive, succeeding to hang on in a maelstrom that is not always of their own creation. They are buffeted and blown around but manage to cling on, never beaten. They can take it, they survive. Kathy Kirby is a survivor.

I will leave you with the words from a letter recently received from an admirer who has only just discovered her catalogue of work. From Sweden, Erik wrote: "Kathy, I just wanted to acknowledge one of the greatest voices of the last century."

She need do no more, the legacy is safe.

'As years go rolling by
My whole life through.
I give my love, and all
My thanks to you'

(Gay, Newell)

PYE
7N.15313 Love Can Be/Crush Me (1960)
7N.15342 Danny/Now You're Crying (1961)

DECCA
F.11505 Big Man/Slowly (1962)
F.11682 Dance On/Playboy (1963)
F.11759 Secret Love/You Have To Want To Love Him (1963)
F.11832 Let Me Go Lover/The Sweetest Sounds (1964)
F.11892 You're The One/Love Me Baby (1964)
F.11992 Don't Walk Away/No Regrets (1964)
F.12087 I Belong/I'll Try Not To Cry (1965)
F.12177 The Way Of Love/Oh Darling, How I Miss You (1965)
F.12280 Where In The World/That Wonderful Feeling Of Love (1965)
F.12338 Spanish Flea/Till The End Of Time (1966)
F.12432 Adam Adamant/Will I Never Learn (1966)
F.13228 Can't Help Lovin' That Man/Bill (1971 – Album.Stars & Garters)
F.11759 Secret Love/You Have To Want To Touch Him (1963 –

re-issued 1981)

COLUMBIA
DB.8139 No One's Gonna Hurt You/My Yiddishe Momma (1967)
DB.8192 In All The World/Time (1967)
DB.8302 Turn Around/Golden Days (1967)
DB.8400 I Almost Called Your Name/Let The Music Start (1968)
DB.8521 Come Back Here With My Heart/Antonio (1968)
DB.8559 I'll Catch The Sun/Please Help Me I'm Falling (1969)
DB.8634 Is That All There Is/Knowing When To Leave (1969)
DB.8721 My Way/Little Green Apples (1970)
DB.8682 Wheel Of Fortune/Lucky (1970)
DB.8795 So Here I Go/Yes – I've Got (1971)
DB.8910 Do You Really Have A Heart/Dream On, Dreamer (1972)
DB.8965 Here, There And Everywhere/Little Song For You (1973)

ORANGE
OAS.216 Singer With The Band/Hello Morning (1973)

PRESIDENT
PT.455 My Prayer/Nobody Loves Me Like You Do (1976)
PT.491 He/Nobody Loves Me Like You Do (1981/1976)

EXTENDED PLAY (DECCA RELEASES)
DFE.8537 "Kathy Kirby" (1963)
                    Big Man/Playboy/Dance On/Love Me Baby
DFE.8596 "Kathy Kirby Volume 2" (1964)
                    Shangrila/That Old Feeling/Reach Out For Me/
                    There's No Other Love
DFE.8611 "A Song For Europe" (1965)
                    I Belong/I'll Try Not To Cry/One Day/Sometimes/
                    My Only Love/I Won't Let You Go

FEATURED COMPILATION ALBUMS
PYE Golden Guinea GGL.0252 "Stars from Stars and Garters" (1964)
                    Danny/Just Say I Love Him/Can't Say Goodbye
DECCA LK.4695 "14 Great Artistes" Lords Taverners Charity Album (1965)
                    Soon I'll Wed My Love

(Secret Love and the Decca hits are featured on many compilation albums
of the 1960's including 'Ready Steady Go', 'Thank Your Lucky Stars',
'Saturday Club' and 'Hit Girls Of The 1960's)

ALBUMS
DECCA LK4575 "16 Hits From Stars and Garters (1963)
   Let Me Sing And I'm Happy/I Can't Give You Anything But Love/
Someone To Watch Over Me/I'll Get By/Acapulco22 /Following In
Father's Footsteps/Waiting For The Robert E.Lee/Bill/Happy Days and
Lonely Nights/Who's Sorry Now/Can't Help Lovin' Dat Man/If You
Were The Only Boy In The World/The Man I Love/Miss Dynamite/On
The Sunny Side Of The Street/Show Me The Way To Go Home.
DECCA LK.4746 "Make Someone Happy" (1965)
   My Man/Happiness Is A Thing Called Joe/Body And Soul/I Want To
Be Happy/I Wish Your Love/Make Someone Happy/Ol'Man Moses/
Sometimes I'm Happy/Havah Nagilah /Happiness Street/My Heart Sings.

ACE OF CLUBS
ACL.1235 "Best Of Kathy Kirby" (1967)
Secret Love/Body And Soul/Big Man/Shangrila/Acapulco 22/Spanish
Flea/Havah Nagilah/My Man/No Regrets/Let Me Go Lover/The Way
Of Love/Dance On.

COLUMBIA
SX.6259 "My Thanks To You" (1968)
You Do Something To Me/More Than You Know/It Only Happens When I Dance With You/I'll Always Love You/I Wanna Be Loved By You/ Thinking Of You/You Brought A New Kind Of Love To Me/If I Loved You/You Were Meant For Me/You My Love/Always True To You In My Fashion/My Thanks To You.

DECCA
SPA.84 "The World Of Kathy Kirby" (1970)Secret Love/Following In Father's Footsteps/Let Me Go Lover/Bill/Playboy/Dance On/Don't Walk Away/The Way Of Love/ Big Man/Spanish Flea/Acapulco 22/Bye Bye Birdie.

PRESIDENT
PLE.507 (LP & Cassette) "Let Me Sing And I'm Happy"
                    (1983 re-issue of 16 Hits From Stars and Garters)

CDs
LONDON 8206282 "Secret Love" (1989)
EMI EMS.1452 "The Best Of The EMI Years" (1992)
SPECTRUM 5520972 "The Very Best Of Kathy Kirby" (1997)
David Innes (mail order) "The Long Lost Shows" (2000)
VOCALION CDLK.4215 "Hits, Rarities and Lipgloss" (2003)
VOCALION CDLK4239 "My Thanks to You" (2005)
SPECTRUM 9824795 "Kathy Kirby, The Complete Collection" (2005)

**Read what Kathy's fans from around the
world have said on her web site at
www.kathykirby.co.uk**

To Kathy, my fellow Libra
I remember hearing your magnificent voice for
the first time in the sixties, while in my teens, and it was the classic
performance of The Way Of Love which I ran out and purchased
on a 45rpm and it still sounds as great today on DVD!!! A voice of
such magnificence is timeless in its beauty and I hope that a time
comes when you share your wonderful gift again...but for now I
am enjoying all of the great CD releases of your wonderful work!
Your gorgeous version of Body And Soul is the definitive version
without a doubt!!! Love and best wishes to you,
Bradly Briggs~Toluca Lake, California

Have enjoyed many happy hours with Kathy's music, seen her
many times in various shows over the years, on the Isle of Man
London Blackpool Bristol, Devon. Come back Kathy we all love
you and wish you lots of love.
Brian Keenan

Would love to get reacquainted. Met when I was backing vocalist
with Roy Orbison on his UK Tours back in the 60s. spoke with
you an exchanged details at I think Hammersmith Odeon when on
the same show. Had a good conversation. Love to hear from you
direct.
David Montanna

Love the site. I would gladly spend all my pink pounds on buying Kathy Kirby albums. Kathy is a gay icon and young folk like myself are finding her music refreshing. I've been a fan for three years and have just found it.Can't wait for the book and TV series . Thank you so much Kathy for your music. You're a real star, not like the rubbish we're expected to put up with today. I know at least five people of my age who are now looking forward to the book. And if you were to ever sing again in public I would be sure to be there,but then again if your happy living a private life we will still love you the same.

God bless you Kathy and be happy

Derek Connor

As a fan of Kathy since the 60s, it was great to come across this web site on the internet. I saw Kathy perform at the Darlington Hotel in Ayr in the 70s and she was sensational. I now live in Melbourne and the only time I hear Kathy mentioned is when one of our local stations plays one of her oldies. It is great to have this link to one of my favourite singers.

Norma Randall

Kathy, you where sensational with film star looks,and a lovely voice, I adored your singing in the 60s and still do, the singers of today could learn a lot from you,be happy, you deserve it.

Mel Warburton

What a great singer. I remember Kathy performing on Stars and Garter, and my parents never missed the show. beautiful and talented.....how sad Kathy deprived us all of her great voice and beautiful presence.

Anna Goodall

Secret Love has and always will be my favourite song of all time. Thanks for introducing a song I love to sing, alone, loud and best of all, on my own. Long live lip gloss, a girls best friend!
Susan Burgess

It is great to see that I am NOT the only Kathy Kirby fan under 30!
If only someone could tempt Miss Kirby to perform on stage again. That is something I would be very pleased to see.
Good luck Miss Kirby, in whatever you choose to do!
David Przeworski

As a child my Dad was mad on Kathy Kirby, that was in the 60s. I remember her as a glamorous lady and my Dad loved her. He died aged 75 on 13th June 2005 and Secret Love was played at his funeral. It was truly moving. You seem to have a new lease of life Kathy, as everyone one , young and old loved it., Thanks for the wonderful memories. Love, hope you are well.
Tib Fodor

Kathy, if you read this PLEASE come back to us. I have missed you desperately and no other singer has taken your place. Your talent is limitless. You were treated very badly and kicked when you were down. Please remember that people still love you and would be ecstatic at your return to the stage, where you reign supreme.
Love
Gerald

I was so thrilled to see a CD of Kathy's in a shop in Eastbourne on Sunday that I immediately bought it . For the next 2 hours I listened to it in the car on the journey back home. It is a dazzling CD and contains all my favourite songs. I loved her in the 60s/70s. A great singer with such oomph! I know of no female artist today who comes anywhere near to being as perfect in voice as Kathy's; a singer who unquestionably deserves much more credit. Additionally, she has been my make-up inspiration, red lips and lip gloss!
Penny

Excellent (naturally) review of The Complete Collection in the May/June issue of HMV Choice magazine. "...and Kathy's distinctive interpretations and warm, strong vocals across the whole delicious experience serve to remind us what a first class singer she was. It's just a pity that Kirby chooses not to perform these days, but this collection will go a long way towards keeping her singular talent alive and kicking."
Ian Parkes

I came across Kathy's song "Dance On" purely by chance a couple of weeks ago (it was a bit before my time) and I can't stop listening to it ever since. What a song! What a voice! Many, many thanks to you Kathy for this and all your other songs I managed to find so far. Can't wait to get my hands on "Spanish Flea" and "Tijuana Taxi". Lots of love and all the best for the future from a true fan.
Simos Papadopoulos

I think all my friends and I were all just a bit in love with Kathy in my road in those early years! Glad to here she's still around.
Love & Best wishes
Charles

This is a great site dedicated to the best female vocalist of the 1960s and beyond...All good wishes to Kathy and James Harman for putting this site together.
Clive Fuller

What a fabulous singer, Many thanks Kathy.
Eric Voice

Excellent website. Kathy was and probably still is a brilliant singer (superb voice). Stay well Kathy we love you.
Bob Brown

Hi, terrific website! I recently bought 'My Thanks To You' and haven't stopped playing it since. Lovely memories. I was lucky enough to see Kathy perform when I was on holiday in Paignton way back. I had been a fan for years and it was the highlight of the holiday and of the year! I wish the years since had been kinder Kathy, but you certainly touched many hearts in the golden years, and you've never been forgotten.
Peter Bellamy